# Learning Organizations

# Learning Organizations

## Turning Knowledge into Actions

Marcus Goncalves

businessexpert
Press

First published in 2012 by
Business Expert Press, LLC
222 East 46th Street, New York, NY 10017
www.businessexpertpress.com

ISBN-13: 978-1-60649-458-5 (paperback)

ISBN-13: 978-1-60649-459-2 (e-book)

DOI 10.4128/9781606494592

Business Expert Press Strategic Management collection

Collection ISSN: 2150-9611 (print)
Collection ISSN: 2150-9646 (electronic)

Cover design by Jonathan Pennell
Interior design by Exeter Premedia Services Private Ltd., Chennai, India

First edition: 2012

10 9 8 7 6 5 4 3 2 1

Printed in the United States of America.

To my forever beautiful wife, Carla, my son Samir living here on earth, and my children Andrea and Joshua, which are now living in Heaven. To God be the glory!

Marcus Goncalves, Spring 2012

# Abstract

In a world that's facing economic recession, more and more professionals, teams, organizations, and inter-organizational networks are facing the need to restructure and renew themselves with the primary purpose of profitably trading their knowledge to add even higher value to their bottom line. Knowledge management has become a key strategic asset for the 21st century economy, and for every organization that values knowledge, it must invest in developing the best strategy for identifying, developing, and applying the knowledge assets it needs to succeed; it must strive to become a learning organization. To remain competitive every organization must invest in creating and implementing the best knowledge networks, processes, methods, tools, and technologies. This will enable them to learn, create new knowledge, and apply the best knowledge much faster.

The aim of this book is to provide readers with key information necessary to become more successful with knowledge creating, transfer, and management, ultimately turning themselves and their organizations into a learning organization.

# Keywords

knowledge management, knowledge capital, tacit knowledge, learning organizations, knowledge technologies

# Contents

# Acknowledgments

There were many people who helped me during the process of writing this book. It would be impossible to keep track of them all. Therefore, to all that I have forgotten to list, please don't hold it against me!

I would like to thank Olivier Serrat, Principal Knowledge Management Specialist at the Asian Development Bank, for graciously allowing me to use some of his ideas and diagrams assessing KM investment. I would also like to express my appreciation to many corporate leaders who shared their views and experiences with me about KM at their organizations or their expert insights. My special thanks go to the following leaders: Donald Eastlake III, from Motorola; Larry Miller, from PPL Montana; James Willey, of Pearl Energy of the Philippines; Mark Payne, of International Paper in the United States; David Mellor, from Oracle; and Susan Osterfelt, from Bank of America.

Most importantly, my deepest gratitude to my wife, Carla, sons Samir and Josh (in memory), and my princess and daughter, Andrea (also in memory), for the inspiration they are to me in striving to make a positive difference in this world. I could not forget Ninigapa (in memory of Paganini, the previous bird), my talkative parakeet!

# Introduction

This book is about a much-needed new breed of knowledge workers. Today's knowledge worker, especially in the manufacturing industry, must be able to develop and deliver a rich set of action-oriented tools and procedures that help companies to transition from learning into action, so they can deal with the realities and challenges. In the process, knowledge workers must be able to tap into not only their corporate employees' fact and observations, but also their hopes, fears, dreams, and feelings, so they can then use it to break the major obstacles to action that confront business professionals and organizations.

**Chapter One**, *Challenges Faced by Knowledge Workers in the Global Economy*, addresses the challenges knowledge workers face in a much integrated global economy, where their role is not often well defined and many times confused with those of a CTO with business and information systems skills, or from a different angle, as of a CIO with business and information technology expertise.

**Chapter Two**, *A Knowledge Worker Profile*, focuses on the importance of KM initiatives and how essential a new breed of knowledge workers are, given the increasing dependence of most companies on information and technologies within a business environment of radical, discontinuous change, often at global levels. Although knowledge workers are, and will continue to be, very important in multibillion-dollar KM implementations, these professionals should not let the technology dominate their attention, focusing instead in becoming agents of change.

**Chapter Three**, *Turning Knowledge into Action*, focuses on transferring learning into action. This chapter focuses on the need for organizations to always attempt to bridge their knowledge gap, the gap between know-how and how-to. Knowledge workers must be able to identify, capture, and transfer *learning into action*, not only data or information, being able to identify the knowledge to be captured by breaking up a great percentage of its processes. They should then be able to capture and transfer it to others. But a certain amount of any knowledge, about anything, always remains tacit, and cannot be read or taught. At this level, knowledge is transferred by learning, watching, and trying to experience it. Tacit knowledge is always deeply embedded in the person who performs the task.

**Chapter Four**, *Nurturing Learning Organizations*, draws upon learning to learn, and an effective element of such organizations is the transferring of the knowledge learned. Here, a wealthy perspective of a learning organization is placed in a coherent framework, which is brought to life by an array of engaging and practical examples. Organizations can only achieve performance by constant learning and refocusing of their business strategies and actions. This chapter shows how important it is for knowledge workers to help knowledge managers, and themselves, to dissociate the technology from KM. Technology and document management is only part of the knowledge-transferring program so necessary to extract capital knowledge.

**Chapter Five**, *Knowledge Technologies,* recommends the development of an enterprise system, anchored on organizational information and knowledge technologies, as a platform for organizing knowledge, know-how and data sharing. This chapter not only discusses the benefits and advantages enterprise systems bring to KM, but also emphasizes the fact that such implementation should be a result of a business, rather than a technology decision; otherwise, it may be doomed for failure.

**Chapter Six**, *Having a Mindset of Knowledge Capital*, provides an overview of how knowledge capital has become a valuable asset at organizations and addresses the importance of being able to measure and preserve such an asset. This chapter also addresses issues dealing with knowledge gap at organizations and how to turn knowledge into action.

**Chapter Seven**, *Knowledge Gaps and the Corporate Instinct*, discusses the challenges faced by management in fostering a learning organization, dealing with knowledge gaps, and capitalizing on the opportunities to transcend, renew, and reinvent themselves.

**Chapter Eight**, *Bridging the Knowledge Gap and Leadership Dilemmas*, discusses the need to create knowledge gaps so that an organization can develop disruptive knowledge and promote innovations for competitive advantage. Once an organization becomes more of an instinctive one, there is even a greater need for new knowledge gaps.

# CHAPTER 1

# Challenges Faced by Knowledge Workers in the Global Economy

Until recently, the business-critical value of knowledge management (KM) investment was all but assumed, and experts on the subject all realized that their assumptions were wrong. Many predicted, and are still predicting, that KM and its derived career paths are doomed to extinction. In fact, more than ten years ago, during the spring of 2001, *CIO* magazine commented that KM systems (KMS) didn't work, in particular due to the fact that no one in the organization would use or support such systems, beginning with upper management. And they were right!

Fast forward to the financial meltdown of 2008 and we realized that very few companies have escaped the impact of the past year's economic woes. Even those organizations that have not been forced to implement redundancy programs have had to implement widespread budgetary cuts, some asking employees to take sabbaticals or part-time work, until economic conditions improve. With resources tight, and internal departments in a state of flux, the case for KM has become even trickier. While KM is normally seen as a *support* service, KM teams may have been among the first to have been culled in recessionary conditions.

But interesting enough, through my consulting practices, those companies that view KM as essential, and central, to business profitability have been more reluctant to make cuts, PPL Montana is a good example of it, as they continue to invest in its people and knowledge capital, and are being very successful at it. In my experience, only a few KM teams have passed through the recession completely unscathed trough.

The theory that a KMS was only as good as its information technology has been nearly unquestionable. But I believe the thinking behind this theory is murky. For the past five years or so, the resounding message from all sectors—professional services firms, corporates and public sector alike—is that KM is now about doing more with less.

The problem is that, as companies focus on building knowledge database repositories and data mining techniques, the majority of them ignore their people and their cultural issues. I believe the massive investments in KM projects in the first decade of the 21st century were thought to underlie the historical globalization, merger and acquisition (M&A) activities across the globe that characterized the 90s. Technology is again becoming one of the most active M&A sector during the past couple of years, much as in the late 1990s, as Figure 1.1 shows.[1] Consequently, the need for information sharing among disparate systems and knowledge base ones were too great, even though the objective evidence for such a claim is controversial at best, but nevertheless, KM has had a free ride for at least the last three or four years.

## The Role of KM

The question we might ask in attempting to define the role of KM is not simple. Was KM the hot topic of yesterday? Is business sustainability now the hot topic of today? Are they different, or is *sustainability* an expansion of the KM concept?

The American Productivity & Quality Center (APQC) describes KM as a mindset that extends beyond the flow of traditional business process. It focuses on the dissemination of information, engagement of key

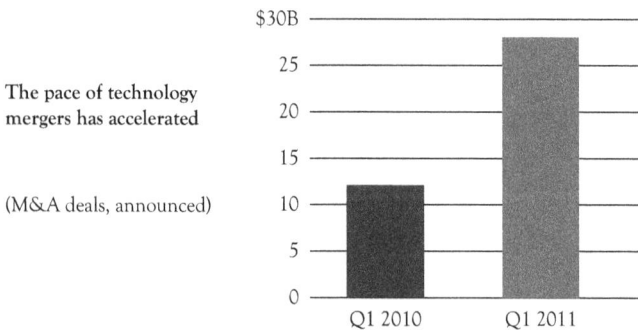

*Figure 1.1. Technology is the most active M&A sector since 2010.*

Source: Ernst & Young's Global technology M&A update: January–March 2012 report.

resources, and ultimately the adoption rate of best practices across the entire value chain. I believe KM and sustainability concepts to be intricately aligned, a critical aspect of business sustainability.

But, the ability to define, implement and manage future business opportunities will depend largely on the availability and quality of critical business information such as:

- Mission: What are we trying to accomplish?
- Competition: How do we gain a competitive edge?
- Performance: How do we deliver the results?
- Change: How do we cope with change?

The bottom line is that the era of KM accountability has come, and corporate KM systems will be judged on the basis of their ability to deliver quantifiable competitive advantage, capable of making your business smarter, faster, and more profitable. In the process, the need to sell the KM concept to employees shouldn't be underestimated. In a fast-paced global economy, knowledge workers should strive to promote an environment where an individual's knowledge is valued and rewarded, establishing a culture that recognizes tacit knowledge and encourages everyone to share it. How we go about it is the challenge.

The old practice of employees being asked to surrender their knowledge, and experience the very traits that makes them valuable as individuals must change. Knowledge cannot be captured; if so, it dies. Thus, motivating employees to contribute to KM activities through implementation of incentive programs is frequently ineffective. Often, employees tend to participate in such programs solely to earn incentives, without regard to the quality or relevance of the information they contribute.

The main challenge here is that KM is overwhelmingly a cultural undertaking. Before setting the course for a KM project and deciding on KM technologies, you will have to know what kinds of knowledge your organization's employees need to share and what techniques and practices should be implemented to get them to share. Thus, you will need a knowledge strategy that reflects and serves as business' goals and attributes. A dispersed, global organization, for example, is probably not well served by a highly centralized knowledge strategy.

To be successful, knowledge workers must be able to implement a very transparent KM activity, one that is focused on simplicity, common sense, and at no time, imposed. Whatever is imposed will always be opposed, which immediately compromises the value and integrity of the knowledge being gathered or shared. Ideally, every employee should desire participation in KM efforts. It should come from within, and its participation should be its own reward. After all, the goal of such initiatives should be to make life easier for employees, therefore positively affecting the bottom line. Otherwise, such effort has failed.

No doubt KM can revolutionize corporation's capital knowledge and sharing. But it won't be easy, and is not likely to be cheap, as the challenges are many, and breaking down user's resistance is one of the major challenges knowledge workers face. You just don't get moving just by buying and installing one of the many KM applications already available on the market. One must have a deeper understanding of the reason, the context and the business challenges being addressed. Therefore, in general knowledge workers are responsible for:

- Strategic issues related to learning, business intelligence, customer relationships, intellectual assets, and agility.
- Influencing, building and changing organizational culture, practices and policies to enable greater innovation, knowledge sharing and creativity.
- Introducing advanced practices to improve knowledge creation and sharing, such as, tools for building a corporate memory, enabling virtual forums, stewarding communities of practice, assisting with informal learning.

Knowledge managers are also expected to engage and mentor executives in the finer points of KM—creating open space, building trust, showing a tolerance for learning via errors, helping with hiring qualities that promote knowledge flows. Depending on circumstances, they may be involved with knowledge audits and mapping, development of taxonomic policy, decisions on software procurement and adoption and will be expected to lead the firm in working with tacit knowledge assets.

There are many more roles and competencies, but I would recommend that you to spend quality time planning the KM strategy, and be forewarned that the initiative may be expensive, not only in terms of capital investments but also in terms of human resource and organizational investments. With that in mind, you will be able to better plan for it. You should begin with the challenges discussed here. Then, you should focus on the many strategies outlined throughout this book, which affect, not only IT support, but also cultural and business issues, and ultimately the role of the knowledge worker as catalyst and flagship of the whole process.

## Implementing KM

The ultimate goal of a knowledge worker should be to bridge the gap between a corporation's know-how and its how-to. Even if a KM implementation is successful from the technical, usability, knowledge aggregation and retrieval view, empowering the organization to transform its know-how into how-to is still virtually a utopian task. But I'm a believer that the definition of success equals vision in action. Seeking business success, several companies undertake tremendous reengineering cycles and hire expensive consultants to tell them what they often already know, and have known for years, after reports and more reports generated by a number of management and business consulting firms.

You might have a clear vision of your KM project goals, but if you don't have a clear action plan in place, one that can be measured using reliable metrics, you just won't succeed. By the same token, you may have a clear action plan, one that very likely has been outlined, developed, and recommended in-house, or by outside consultants, but if you don't have a clear vision of where you are going, the results you want to achieve, you just won't get there either.

Don't underestimate the complexity of KM implementations. If you look at enterprise resource planning (ERP) and customer relationship management (CRM) solutions you can have some idea. But very few ERP implementations have been fully successful; most of them are still under the implementation phase, being clogged up with CRM solutions, or already undergoing some level of business process rethinking. The same goes for CRM. According to Mendoza, Marius, Pérez, & Grimán (2007) survey results, the main causes of CRM project failures have to do with organizational change (29%), company policies/inertia (22%), little understanding of CRM (20%) and poor CRM skills (6%). Mind you, CRM success results are much more tangible to measure than KM ones!

What those surveys underline is an increasing skepticism about intelligent systems. Knowledge workers must be able to avoid, if not eliminate, them. To get 100 percent satisfaction in KM implementations is not only very expensive, but near to impossible. It's not enough to install a KM system. You need to convince your people to use it, starting with upper management.

In addition, immediate results are near nonexistent, until users are able to feed the system with all their best practices, explicit knowledge, and whatever knowledge they believe can earn them the announced motivational perk. Of course, you can always mention the success of the KM system used by British Petroleum sharing knowledge through its virtual team network.[2] The aim of that system was to allow people to work cooperatively and share knowledge quickly and easily regardless of time, distance, and organizational boundaries. The network is a rapidly growing system of sophisticated personal computers equipped so that users can work together as if they were in the same room and can easily tap the company's rich database of information. The PCs boast videoconferencing capability, electronic blackboards, scanners, faxes, and groupware. Amazingly enough, today's knowledge worker's challenges are much broader in scope, as well as influential. The following are the most important ones.

## Technology-Driven KM Challenges

KM and learning are both evolving practices enhancing individual's learning and understanding through provision of information. KMS are normally characterized as technologies to provide and access information. However, the pedagogical approaches used are more important than the procedural features of the technology. Thus, one of the main challenges of knowledge technologies relates to the pedagogical approach in implementing and using such systems. It is important to adopt a knowledge-based pedagogical (KBP) framework that highlights the involvement of KM across the organizations. There are still many unanswered questions concerning the part that knowledge plays in decision-making and key challenges to integrate customer's value, evidence and choice into a KM system. This, I believe, is due to lack of pedagogical practices on assessing the value of knowledge, comprehension and learning applications.

A mistake several organizations continue to make with KM initiatives is to think of it as a technology-based concept. There are no all-inclusive KM solutions and any software or system vendor touting such concept is either deceived or grossly misinformed. To implement solely technology-based systems such as electronic messaging, Web portals, centralized databases, or any other collaborative tool, and think you have implemented a KM program is not only naïve, but also a waste of time and money.

Of course, technology is a major KM enabler, but it is not the end, and not even the starting point of a KM implementation. A sound KM program should always start with two indispensable and cheap tools: pencil and paper. The knowledge worker's challenge here is to plan, plan and plan. KM decisions must be based on strategies defined by the acronym W3H (who, what, why, and how), or the people, the knowledge, the business objectives, and the technology, respectively. The technology of choice should only come later.

Another challenge that tends to be technology driven is knowledge flow, which is often a stumbling block in most KM programs, and the big mistake knowledge worker's make is to look at technology as the main solution to support the flow of knowledge. Knowledge flow is a much more complex issue, which involves the process of creation and dissemination of new knowledge, as well as human motivation, personal and social construction of knowledge, and virtualization of organizations and communities. I believe knowledge flow is only sustained by the human desire to make sense—common sense that is—of issues that transcend the everyday business scope, but it is very much present in every moment of a professional's life, no matter what his or her trades are.

Every day, as we assimilate, store and disseminate knowledge, organized or not, we are trying to make sense of issues that relate to our interests, passions, lives, work and even family. No technology system can capture such unstructured and tacit knowledge. Trying to do so, instead of supporting its flow, stops it. The situation becomes even more complex when we consider the cultural aspects so present in multinational organizations, especially those that have gone through a merger with foreign companies.

Common sense should also apply to business processes. Most of our business reasoning and purposes are built around a process of justifications for what we would like to do in order to satisfy a business requirement (or is it in order to satisfy ourselves?). In this process, knowledge workers should be aware of tacit knowledge present by virtue of previous experiences in every employee, as well as their studies, thinking, cultural background, while they attempt to verbalize it in form of their responses. Technology alone won't help you in this process.

## Addressing the Challenges

KM is without a doubt an oxymoron that explains the difficulty in reconciling the soft issues around it, such as innovation and creativity, with hard issues, such as performance benchmarks' measurement and assessment. There is a diametrically opposed assumption about the definition and nature between knowledge and management, but for a knowledge worker, management and control are not synonymous, as it would be for a CTO or a CIO.

To cope with the challenges knowledge workers face in organization is not an easy task. Today's knowledge worker's roles are still not well defined, many times confused with those of a CTO with business and information systems skills, or from a different angle, as of a CIO with business and information technology expertise. Much of it is because the role of a knowledge worker in today's organizations falls into a *demilitarized zone* between the organization and information systems, as depicted in Figure 1.2.

As a result of this super information overflow, KM initiatives are often disappointing, as there is a lack of user uptake and a failure to integrate KM into everyday working practices. However, such outcome can be avoided, and this is what this whole book is all about. Make sure to tighten your KM efforts to high-priority business objective—just as you wouldn't fish in a pond with a bazooka, don't invest in KM just for KM's sake. To be successful, knowledge and learning goals must be

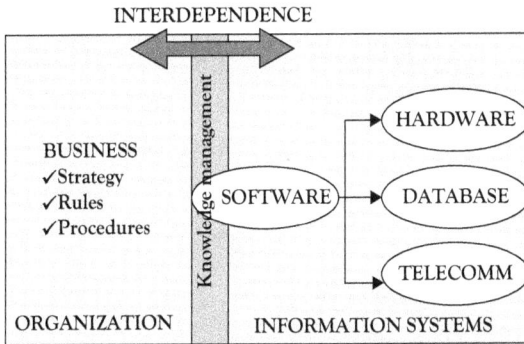

*Figure 1.2. KM is the only discipline with a real chance to manage the systems interdependencies between the organization and information systems.*

articulated at the same level of an organization's business objectives. This is the only way learning and knowledge sharing can truly become culturally embedded in the organization. If you want KM to succeed, you must integrate your people with the organization's business process and the technology you will be using—KM should always be a work-in-progress, never a finite project. Its never-ending integrated process should always be the implementation of a competitive strategy, which appreciates that learning and sharing knowledge are equally important.

Implementing KM is not as easy as we would like it to be. Really, you only have one shot, and if this fails, you may find that the concept has become irrecoverably tarnished. Therefore, before even thinking about the implementation of KM you must devise a plan based on lessons from successful (and not so successful!) implementations in other organizations, and adapted to your own corporate needs.

A sound KM implementation plan should be based on:

- The results of assessment and benchmarking (if available);
- A KM strategy (if available);
- The proposed and agreed KM framework (if available);
- A communications plan (if available);
- A staged, change management approach;
- A full analysis of the risks to KM delivery.

In addition, when considering a KM implementation, make sure to have a knowledge strategy aligned with your organization's business strategy way before considering any technology tool. And make sure the strategy defines all key KM processes:

- Creation of new knowledge
- Identification of knowledge
- Capturing of knowledge
- Knowledge mapping
- Knowledge sharing, application and reuse
- Protection and security of knowledge assets.

## Chapter Summary

In this chapter we discussed the challenges faced by knowledge workers in the global economy. We addressed the new roles KM must embrace to address the challenges of a heterogeneous global business environment, as well as the factors involved in the implementation of KM at organizations, particularly the technology driven ones.

# CHAPTER 2

# A Knowledge Worker Profile

At the time of these writings, spring of 2012, the economy in United States is in a major downturn. Some analyst would say the country is in a recession, while others would disagree. Either way, the slowing economy, which transcends across the American borders into the European Union and beyond, is giving a new blow to knowledge worker-lead KM project teams.

Today's knowledge workers, and KM professionals for that matter, are required to change their business structure and the way their KM implementations are managed to enable their projects to remain under budget, meet deadlines, and most important, pay off. Focusing on knowledge sharing, Internet-based applications and virtual access to data, knowledge workers are emerging as a driving force in the collaborative implementation of KM. However, given the high risk for KM implementation failures, the new breed of knowledge workers required to lead such teams must have a multitude of skills, including business, technology, team-building, project management, communication skills, and leadership in order to be successful.

In the words of Rebecca Barclay,[1] these new breed of knowledge workers must possess *vision, strategy, ambassadorial skills, and a certain je ne sais quoi.* This is true especially when we consider the traditional methods of calculating return on investment (ROI), which are often ill-suited to measuring the strategic impact of KM applications and initiatives, in particular those applied to customer-facing systems such as CRM. That's because KM can have a profound strategic impact on a company, far beyond improving processes and productivity. KM can fundamentally change the way a company view its business, its products and even its business opportunities.

Knowledge workers or *infoknowledgist* are workers whose main capital is knowledge. Typical examples may include software engineers, architects, engineers, scientists, and lawyers, because they "think for a living."[2]

What differentiates knowledge work from other forms of work is its primary task of "nonroutine" problem solving that requires a combination of convergent, divergent, and creative thinking.[3] The issue of who knowledge workers are, and what knowledge work entails, however, is still debated. One might consider a definition of knowledge work which includes, "all workers involved in the chain of producing and distributing knowledge products," which allows for an incredibly broad and inclusive categorization of knowledge workers. It should thus be acknowledged that the term "knowledge worker"[4] can be quite broad in its meaning, and is not always definitive in who it refers to.

Therefore, the need for a new breed of knowledge worker's, ones that must redefine their roles and become more business focused, is evident. In addition to possessing business acumen, this new breed of knowledge worker also must be able to approach KM ROI with a new view, one toward establishing both an initial justification for projects, and a very clear baseline for ongoing management decisions and incentives. The main goal should be to increase knowledge sharing, with very specific deliverables, including but not limited to:

- Cultivating employee satisfaction, which should lead to an enhanced customer service.
- Rising individual and program effectiveness, productivity, and responsiveness.
- Increasing the opportunity for communication and collaboration throughout the organization.
- Crafting knowledge and tools needed to do the work available for sharing via the Internet.
- Fostering innovation as the outcome of sharing of knowledge and best practices.

## Knowledge Workers as Change Agents

KM is for the most part a product of the incredible changes of the 1990s. Economic globalization expanded, bringing about new opportunities and an aggressive increase in competition. As a result, companies reacted to it by downsizing, merging, acquiring, reengineering, and outsourcing their operations. Benefiting from the latest advances in computer information systems and network technology, businesses were able to streamline their workforces and boost up productivity and their profits. Higher profits, low inflation, cheap capital and new technologies all helped fuel the biggest and hottest bull market the U.S. economy had ever seen. Employment levels were at record highs and skilled workers in high demand. Businesses came to understand that by managing their knowledge they could continue to increase profits without expanding the workforce.

It was in face of those challenges that KM began to attract the attention of the federal government, which was also experiencing profound changes during the 1990s. Payrolls were cut by 600,000 positions; the use of information technology was expanded to improve performance, and management reforms were enacted to improve performance and to increase accountability to the American people. KM presents to the government today a major challenge. The federal government faces serious human capital issues as it strives to improve service and be more accountable. It must compete for workers, as its workforce grows older. Employees of the federal government are older on average than workers in the private sector. Fifty-eight percent of all federal employees were aged 45 or older in March 2009, and almost 25% were aged 55 or older. In contrast, only 42% of wage and salary workers in the private sector were 45 or older in 2007, and 18% were 55 or older.[5] This means that unless the knowledge of those leaving is retained, service to citizens will likely suffer.

What all this data means is that executives will no longer be able to rely on information technologies alone to take care of the company's competitive advantage. In addition, organizations will no longer be able to rely on people the way they have been trained in the existing educational, organizational, and business models. In today's global economy, the right answer in one time and context can become wrong solutions in another time and context. By the same token, best practices may become worse practices, unless they are constantly analyzed and revised for their sensibility, which can impair business performance and competence. Thus, the logic of yesterday's success doesn't necessarily dictate the success of today and certainly won't dictate the logic of success for a brand-new tomorrow.

In order to succeed, knowledge workers must adjust their vision and humbly grab a hold of their *je ne sais quoi* and react to it by evaluating and reviewing KM practices and strategies, as a catalyst tool to refocus and reanalyze business data. Believe me, this is just the beginning. In the next five years, information will continue to flow at the speed of light, making it harder and harder for CEOs and senior staff to hold their lines in this supercharged economy. Along with tremendous change in the public and private sectors we see an explosive growth in the Internet and the emergence of e-business and e-government. There is so much information available and pushed at us that at times it is very easy to drown in an information overflow. Yet, the work is changing at such a fast pace that our need for constant and up-to-date knowledge that enables us to respond to rapid changes in the workplace continues to widen every day, every minute. Thus, one of the main challenges knowledge workers face is to seek better ways to help professionals to learn and work smarter. KM is one of the most reliable means to address human capital issues and to take business, and e-business for that matter, to the next level.

KM offers a tremendous edge for business advantage, but only if taken seriously and implemented correctly. Enough of fancy data mining, complex business integration, and strategy meetings lineup and focused on technology and systems to promote KM! I always believed the mantra that *success is vision in action*. Knowledge workers must have a vision of what they need to achieve, without biased influence of technology or past generation information systems models. We must reinvent ourselves, and the KM systems we rely on, all the time.

To remain competitive, a business must focus not only on generating profit but also on educating employees and growing their capabilities to take care of customers' needs. Driving a business from the perspective of knowledge and learning rather than strictly from a financial bottom line will give companies a competitive advantage. Knowledge workers are key professionals in this process. Companies are still underestimating the value of knowledge workers for increasing the competitive advantage of the organization and turning the company into a learning company. Most companies are just starting to realize the value of knowledge workers, most of them within the operating groups, which are beginning to rely on them on marketing calls, pre- and post-sales meetings and high-level interaction with customers and potential customers. Knowledge workers add great value in these areas, as typically they are able to bridge the gap between information, knowledge and a firm's customer base. And, because of their value, they are increasingly being asked to interface with boards of directors as well.

As the speed of business increases, so does the rate of professional turnover inside companies, particularly in the professional service sector. Whenever knowledge walks out of the door organizations need to start projects from ground zero, the value of knowledge workers and KM programs becomes very evident. Lost knowledge takes a tactical toll as companies spend money to re-create it and bring people up to speed. By managing organizational knowledge, a knowledge worker changes organizational culture, people become empowered to make decisions and cycle times are reduced. If you want to find a suitable knowledge worker or if you are wondering yourself if you have the talent it takes, be aware that the best knowledge workers are driven by the challenge of changing how organizations think about knowledge, and about themselves. Knowledge workers are real visionaries, and there is not enough salary, title, or any other corporate perks to motivate them more than the challenge of finding solutions and remaking the thought process that drives them.

### Overcoming Organizational and Behavioral Changes

One of the main challenges KM faces today is with regard to organizational and behavioral changes. These are the most difficult tasks when implementing anything, in particular KM. Implementing technology, buying software, is the least complex variable of the equation. Thus, today's knowledge workers must be aware of these challenges.

In the past, behavioral changes were not taking so much into consideration. Decisions were made from the top-down and all the organizations underneath just adapted to it. Today, organizations are much more decentralized and the global economy and shorter business cycles allow for options people didn't have before. No longer are professionals looking at positions within their companies as permanent. Typically, professionals move around within two to three years. Whatever can be done to minimize turnovers becomes very important, as along with capturing the knowledge of those leaving before they do so.

To this extent, KM professionals are in essence *change agents*, acting as catalysts for change. They should be the ones chosen to bring about organizational change. Corporations often hire senior managers or even chief executives because of their ability to effect change.

## Fostering Change Through Mentoring

As a formal, and often informal, relationship between two people—a senior mentor and a junior protégé, mentoring has been identified as an important influence in professional development in both the public and private sector. The war for talent is creating challenges within organization not only to recruit new talent, but also to retain talent. Benefits of mentoring include increased employee performance, retention, commitment to the organization, and knowledge sharing.

Many organizations run formal stand-alone mentoring programs aimed at enhancing career and interpersonal development. But formal mentoring programs have structure, oversight, and clear and specific organizational goals. Overall, organizations should implement formal mentoring programs for different purposes, including but not limited to:

- To help new employees settle into the agency
- To create a knowledge sharing environment
- To develop mission critical skills
- To help accelerate one's career
- To improve retention.

Mentoring is a good strategy to promote desired organizational behavior. Not only is it a good channel for knowledge transfer, but it is also an effective way to develop loyalty and accountability among professionals, in particular among those being mentored and the ones who mentor them. I often use mentoring strategies to get those being mentored, let's call them disciples, in line and unified with a particular goal at hand and to give them vision. The dynamics invariably work because they feel ownership for the project, an integral part of it. Instead of considering themselves a hired hand (compensated by salaries), mentoring, or discipleship, gives them the vision they need to achieve success.

Over the years, I've seen mentoring evolve from an experimental technique to management strategy to a full-blown cult. Seasoned professionals offer guidance to aspiring entrepreneurs. Wise alumni take uncertain young graduates under their wings. Those who've kicked drugs help addicts who want to quit. Cancer survivors give hope to the newly stricken. Mentorship can be an effective strategy today's knowledge workers can use. However, if you are going to play the role, you need to understand what your disciples need and how to practices the fine art of encouragement. If you can always be a source of encouragement for your organization and teach the employees to do the same, I guarantee you will have a tight team, brought together not for salary, titles, or corporate perks, but for a vision, a dream and the feeling of purpose and self-worth. A small team like this can win big battles!

Keep in mind that mentoring is a communication strategy; it enables individuals to engage in conversations and relationships directed at enhancing career satisfaction, professional development, and professional practice. Mentoring is a longerterm relationship in which someone with more experience and wisdom (mentor) supports and encourages another (mentee/protégé) as that individual grows and develops professionally and personally. In mentoring the focus is mainly on role modeling and guidance rather then on supervision and instruction.

Now, be careful not to turn mentoring into a commodity, and don't let anyone else do it either. The danger in mentoring, as a KM strategy, is that those being mentored tend to believe they should have a mentor who saves them, guides them, and watches out for them for the rest of their careers. In other words, make sure they don't check off. As mentors, knowledge workers may play many roles, from being an active guide and occasional counselor, to a constructive critic. The more hats you can wear, and wear well, the better, but it's rare to find one person who can do all of the above.

### The Five Phase Mentoring Relationship Model

When mentoring groups or even individuals, as depicted in Figure 2.1, there are many techniques to aid you in the process. The Five Mentoring Relationship Model was designed by Donner Wheeler and Integral Visions Consulting[6] to guide mentoring relationships from the establishment of

**Phase one: Purpose**
*Why do I want a mentor?*
*Why do I want to be a mentor?*

**Phase two: Engagement**
Finding and being a mentor
*How do I begin?*

**Phase three: Planning**
Developing your mentoring action plan
*How can I achieve my goals?*
*How will we work together?*

**Phase four: Emergence**
Engaging in the conversation
*How am I doing?*
*What are we learning?*

**Phase five: Completion**
Celebrating accomplishments
*What are my next steps?*

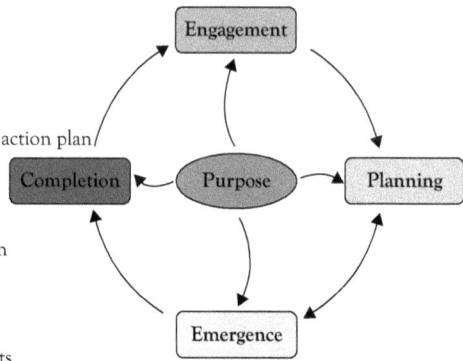

*Figure 2.1. Five phase mentoring relationship model.*

*Source:* Cooper & Wheeler (2007) Building successful mentoring relationships, http://www.donnerwheeler.com/Programs_and_Services/Mentoring, last accessed on 8/1/2012.

the purpose of the mentoring relationship, through engaging the right mentor, establishing a plan for the mentoring, the emergence and ongoing activity of the relationship, and honoring the achievement of goals and completion of the relationship.

Today's knowledge worker should *evangelize* the practice of building mentoring programs into their organization's human resource departments, their own KM group, or even making mentoring a formal responsibility of managers. Make sure that mentors and mentees do have a set time together, where participants discuss expectations and map out how and when to fulfill them. Keep in mind that contact between mentor and mentee is sometimes as informal as a weekly telephone check-in or occasional excursions out of the workplace, where both parties feel free to let down their hair. At the other extreme are programs with written contracts, structured activities such as "shadowing" (where the mentee follows the mentor around for a prescribed period), and formal evaluation of the mentoring relationship by a third party.

Some people are hesitant to approach a mentor for fear of being a drain on their time and energy. However, the high degree of satisfaction in helping someone develop and the pleasure of being exposed to new ideas are always rewarding and responsible for keeping such programs flowing. For their part, mentees learn new skills, new competencies and the complex politics of an organization. And the company gains by boosting motivation and advancement, which leads to greater employee retention. Thus, mentoring is a win-win situation.

Listening is also a very important aspect of mentoring. It involves hearing, sensing, interpreting, evaluating, and responding. Good listening is an essential part of being a good leader, and the cornerstone of this new breed of knowledge workers. You cannot be a good knowledge manager unless you are a good listener. You as a knowledge worker must be very aware of the feedback you are receiving from the people around you. If you are not a good listener, your future as a knowledge worker will be short.

Good listening includes a package of skills, which requires knowledge of technique and practice very similar to good writing or good speaking. In fact, poor listening skills are more common than poor speaking skills. I am sure that you have seen on many occasions two or more people talking to each other at the same time. In improving your listening skills, be aware that there is shallow listening and deep listening. Shallow or superficial listening is all too common in business settings and many other settings. Most of us have learned how to give the appearance of listening to our supervisors, the public speaker, and the chair of the meeting while not really listening. Even less obvious is when the message received is different from the one sent. We did not really understand what the message is. We listened, but we did not get the intended message. Such failed communications are the consequences of poor speaking, poor listening, and/or poor understanding.

The following attributes of good listening are suggestive of the skills needed for a new breed of knowledge workers. There is some overlap between the various attributes, but each suggests something different.

- **Attention**—This is the visual portion of concentration on the speaker. Through eye contact and other body language, we communicate to the speaker that we are paying close attention to his/her messages. All the time we are reading the verbal and nonverbal cues from the speaker, the speaker is reading ours. What messages are we sending out? If we lean forward a little and focus our eyes on the person, the message is we are paying close attention.

- **Concentration**—Good listening is normally hard work. At every moment we are receiving literally millions of sensory messages. Nerve endings on our bottom are telling us the chair is hard, others are saying our clothes are binding, nerve ending in our nose are picking up the smells of cooking French fries, or whatever, our ears are hearing the buzzing of the computer fan, street sounds, music in the background, and dozens of other sounds, our emotions are reminding us of that fight we had with our mate last night, and thousands more signals are knocking at the doors of our senses. Focus your attention on the words, ideas, and feeling related to the subject. Concentrate on the main ideas or points. Don't let examples or fringe comments distract you.
- **Don't Interject**—There is a great temptation at many times for the listener to jump in and say in essence: "Isn't this really what you meant to say." This carries the message: "I can say it better than you can," which stifles any further messages from the speaker. Often, this process may degenerate into a game of one-upmanship in which each person tries to outdo the other and very little communication occurs.
- **Empathy, not sympathy**—Empathy is the action of understanding, being aware of, being sensitive to, and vicariously experiencing the feelings, thoughts and experience of another. Sympathy is having common feelings. In other words as a good listener you need to be able to understand the other person, you do not have to become like them. Try to put yourself in the speaker's position so that you can see what he/she is trying to get at.
- **Eye contact**—Good eye contact is essential for several reasons. By maintaining eye contact, some of the competing visual inputs are eliminated. You are not as likely to be distracted from the person talking to you. Another reason, most of us have learned to read lips, often unconsciously,

and the lip reading helps us to understand verbal messages. Also, much of many messages are in nonverbal form and by watching the eyes and face of a person we pick up clues as to the content. A squinting of the eyes may indicate close attention. A slight nod indicates understanding or agreement. Most English language messages can have several meanings depending upon voice inflection, voice modulation, facial expression, etc.

- **Leave the Channel Open**—A good listener always leaves open the possibility of additional messages. A brief question or a nod will often encourage additional communications

- **Objective**—We should be open to the message the other person is sending. It is very difficult to be completely open because each of us is strongly biased by the weight of our past experiences. We give meaning to the messages based upon what we have been taught the words and symbols mean by our parents, our peers, and our teachers.

- **Receptive Body Language**—Certain body postures and movements are culturally interpreted with specific meanings. The crossing of arms and legs is perceived to mean a closing of the mind and attention. The nodding of the head vertically is interpreted as agreement or assent. Now, be careful, as nonverbal clues such as these vary from culture to culture just as the spoken language does. If seated, the leaning forward with the upper body communicates attention. Standing or seated, the maintenance of an appropriate distance is important. Too close and we appear to be pushy or aggressive, and too far and we are seen as cold.

- **Restating the message**—Your restating the message as part of the feedback can enhance the effectiveness of good communications. Take comments such as: "I want to make sure that I have fully understood your message...." and then paraphrase in your own words the message. If the communication is not clear, such a feedback will allow for immediate clarification. It is important that you state the message as clearly and objectively as possible.

- **Strategic Pauses**—Pauses can be used very effectively in listening. For example, a pause at some points in the feedback can be used to signal that you are carefully considering the message that you are "thinking" about what was just said.
- **Understanding of Communication Symbols**—A good command of the spoken language is essential in good listening. Meaning must be imputed to the words. For all common words in the English language there are numerous meanings. The three-letter word "run" has more than one hundred different uses. You as the listener must concentrate on the context of the usage in order to correctly understand the message. The spoken portion of the language is only a fraction of the message. Voice inflection, body language, and other symbols send messages also. Thus, a considerable knowledge of nonverbal language is important in good listening.
- **You cannot listen while you are talking**—This is very obvious, but very frequently overlooked or ignored. An important question is why are you talking: to gain attention?

In summary, good listening is more than polite silence and attention when others speak, and it's altogether different from manipulative tactics masquerading as skill. It is rather a high virtue, a value and a reflection of bedrock belief that learning what other people have on their mind is a wise investment of one's time.

## Chapter Summary

This chapter focused on the knowledge worker. After addressing the KM environment at organizations and its challenges in chapter one, this chapter provides a profile of the knowledge worker, not necessarily as an information technology professional, but mainly as a change agent. Challenges dealing with organizational and behavioral changes were discussed, as well as the ever-increasing need for fostering change at organizations. A special attention is given to mentoring relationships at learning organizations.

# CHAPTER 3

# Turning Knowledge into Action

What is the big deal about KM, you might ask. KM may be quiet, but it is not dead, as it is just beginning to penetrate the fabric of many businesses, and statistics alone prove it. The problem is that the early, flashy-but-insubstantial applications, such as best practices and lessons learned, for example, have given way to broadly focused initiatives that are transforming the way organizations work, in particular in government circles and fortune 100 corporations. Any change takes time, and for the most part, changes are never amenable to shallow, sensationalistic journalistic treatment. In fact, only the most profound, gifted analysts and writers can comprehend and express them. But the new breed of knowledge workers discussed in Chapter 2 also can, and they are the ones holding the KM flag today!

The value of organizational learning should be recognized, as KM can easily be seen as a key corporate asset that must be leveraged and exploited for competitive purpose. In this emerging, global and rapidly changing market, creative ideas and innovative thinking is essential. Learning organizations have been adopted, at least in theory, by many organizations, but are still not as practical as they should be, and best practices are not easily found. This chapter attempts to provide you with a road map to turn your company into a learning organization, with practical examples that you can apply the next day.

## Developing a Learning Organization

In building and maintaining a learning organization you must look for traits, nurture some of them and eliminate others, so you can bridge the knowledge gap in the organization, to allow a successful knowledge transfer into action, from know-how to how-to.

## Having a Defined Learning Agenda

Any learning organization should have a defined learning agenda. Does yours have one? Does your organization have a clear picture of the knowledge requirements it needs to strive and be successful? Look for these attitudes:

- Does your organization know what it needs to know, regardless of the industry, of the competition, the market capitalization, technology trends, customer profiling and services, production processes, knowledge collaboration, and information gathering?
- Is your organization pursuing these knowledge goals with multiple approaches? Once your organization is able to identify its needs for knowledge, it must pursue it with several approaches, which should not be reduced to training and education alone. It should include experimental ones, research studies via analyst firms or in-house resources, simulations, customer surveys, benchmarking when appropriate, etc.

## Being Open to Dissonant Information

Learning organizations should be open to dissonant and incongruent information, disruptive knowledge, to foster innovation. To bridge the knowledge gap that stops organizations from acting on what they know, or need to know, learning organizations must become simultaneously effective and efficient in their actions. However, this requires a higher level of continuous learning between the leaders who drive the organization, which also includes knowledge workers and not only CEOs, the staff delivering the organization's products or service, and the costumers of this organization. You must look at your organization as a complex adaptive human system, trying to become a generative system, more than just mindless machines or merely structured systems. A learning organization is one that breathes and lives out of paradox, of dissonant information, so learn not to shoot the messengers who bring bad news or raise paradoxical ideas! Your goal is to help the organization flourish in such environment, as a child does in its early stages of life. Be prepared to believe, strive, and guide your organization in doing the same when facing paradoxes such as these:

- You may be losing when winning—When your product is a success, or your processes are working, the tendency is to let it be, not to fix what is not broken. However, if you look back to all the successful stories, those businesses disappeared or were replaced because they have failed to respond to a new challenge. The American automobile industry went through it with the Japanese. Apple Computers committed the same mistake with its Apple and Macintosh lines of computers. What happened to excellent software applications such as WordPerfect, dBase II, III, and IV, Lotus SmartSuite? What happened to Netscape, or better yet Mosaic? Organizations, and their products, will die if they can't keep up with the rate of changes in their industry, and trying to play the new game with the old rules is a recipe for disaster. I've seen several organizations not being able to make sense of pseudo-chaotic—not as chaotic as one might think, but a result of disruptive innovation—information and feedback coming in from a tumultuous global market, and trying to react with obsolete tactics, just to waste capital, people and time, and eventually the eagerness to fight on. That's when you must realize that in today's business, learning organizations must compete and cooperate with their competitors. The either-or solutions no longer will hold.
- Choices as cause—If your company is not adopting a generative learning system, which is discussed in more detail later on in this chapter, then you are relying on adaptive learning systems. Such systems always show patterns that can never be predicted in advance, regardless of the familiarity you have with the inputs. This is because you are relying on a reactive system. Thus, the outcomes are result of mere random choices made by members of the staff or organization. Choice here is synonymous with chance, and chance is the one driving the outcome! How about that for a managerial style?

I hope you will find it as disturbing as I did when I finally accepted this paradox!

• Being reasonable can be limiting—In today's business front, being rational is not necessarily being business savvy. Actually, most entrepreneurs I know or read about use a great amount of intuition in their everyday business decisions. Leaders with tremendous business acumen often feel the advantages that their structural positioning in the business network offers them, and learn how to exploit the stream of opportunities that their position allow to flow in their direction. A key factor here is that professionals must learn to identify these opportunities, use intuition in association with the structures surrounding the business and themselves. For too many CEOs and other senior staff, to rely on intuition and feelings, and try to tie these insights to business structures is too intimidating, to say the least. Most executives are convergent-thinkers, data-rational, reductionist managers to accept such paradoxical management challenges. That's why every business plan has a provision for an exit strategy, which I call the moment when the ostrich puts its head on the sand, and doesn't even know from where the kick came from. Instead, I advocate a more Hellenic posture to business, armed with a breastplate but totally unprotected back, just in case I feel tempted to give my back to business challenges.

• Organizations are not simply structures—Organizations are much more than simple structures, as they suffer the influence of human process energies, both negative and positive. People are the ones driving the organization. If people are energized, the organization will be energized.

To change the behavior of such organizations is a very difficult task and many give up in the process. Actually that's one of the main reason the big six consulting firms keep on returning to the same organizations over and over and telling them through reports and best practices the same things, which basically challenges their status quo and call for changes in those areas. A true learning organization will not avoid discussing sensitive issues and make necessary changes in areas such as dissension in ranks, unhappy customers, pre-emptive moves by the competition, and issues with disruptive and new technologies. Typically, information gathered in these areas are filtered and there is a resistance to deal with them, especially among those in the senior level, who tend to avoid being confronted with ideas that may change their status quo or require them to change or leave their comfort zone.

## Developing an Organization's Learning Agenda

I define success as vision in action (success = vision + action). You must realize that any bad or inept vision very likely won't foster appropriate action, likely lending initiatives to failures. Thus, for learning organizations to be successful they must turn their vision into action. Action without a vision is like sailing uncharted waters without a compass. By the same token, vision without action is just an idea, a dream. Learning organizations should not be only a repository of knowledge. For that, let the universities and business schools do their job.

Learning organizations make sure to act on what they know by taking advantage of new learning and by adapting their behaviors accordingly. If organizations don't use the information they have worked so hard to acquire, how good are they? How good is it if an organization realizes an untapped market but fails to take advantage of it? Therefore, it is very important that a learning organization is aware of what knowledge is, how to identify and capture it, as well as transfer it across the organization, effectively turning it into action. Otherwise, the organization will never grow or succeed.

Figure 3.1 depicts what I call the knowledge gap tornado, which I have developed more than a decade ago. It establishes the necessary steps learning organizations must go through in order to grow their understanding of business and themselves, their weaknesses and strengths. Failure to overcome a step, or stage, brings the organization back to its previous stage, and eventually back to the eye of the knowledge gap tornado, characterized by business and strategic chaos.

Conversely, as the learning organization learns and advances, it goes through several growing stages and eventually closes the learning circle,

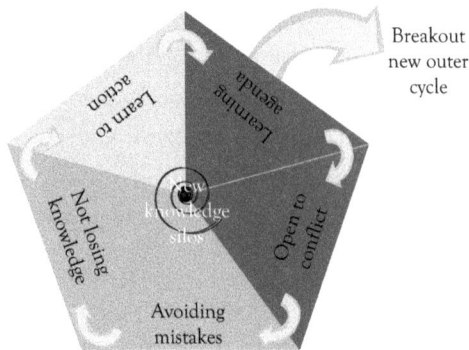

*Figure 3.1. The knowledge [gap] tornado.*

only to restart it again with a new learning agenda, but this time with much more business wisdom than before, allowing it to tap into silos of knowledge that prepare and sustain the organization to the next level of its growth, in an outer circle around the tornado. This process is ever evolving and can be broken down as follows.

### Learning Agenda

As depicted in Figure 3.1, the first step in becoming a learning organization is to have a learning agenda. Otherwise, what you have is an adaptive organization, bowing with the wind of business, rolling with the punches of the competition.

If your organization has a learning agenda, as discussed earlier in this chapter, then it will be ready to move on to the next stage, being open to conflicts.

### Open to Conflicts

At this stage, the learning organization will face a lot of conflicts, as several senior staff members, and the organization as a whole, will face the conflicts with different and individual agendas. To avoid these conflicts can be fatal for the organization. If anything, it will bring the organization back to its first stage, where a learning agenda needs to be redefined or truly established. However, if the organization is open to conflicts, even with the acceptable differences, goals and mission statements, it can deal with the conflicts and get a unified set of goals for the company as a whole. Once senior staff and the remainder of the organization are unified in their understanding of what they are, where they are and where they want to go, as well as what it will take to get them there, then the organization is ready to move to the next step, which is avoiding mistakes.

### Avoiding Mistakes

This is an equally important stage. At this point, learning organizations should have a well-defined learning agenda. They should know where they are heading, and have a plan to get there. The organization also should have purged the inefficiencies afflicting its goals and resolve any conflicts it has with members of the team. Now, it is time to avoid the mistakes of the past, and learn from current mistakes so as to avoid them in the future. Failure to do so will inevitably bring the organization back to the previous step, being open to conflict, as invariably this is the cause for recurring mistakes, either because they were not dealt with in the past or because there was a conflict avoidance when dealing with them, which prevented the organization from learning from its mistakes. Beware that once an organization steps back into a previous stage, the lack of momentum and increased inertia tends to bring the organization all the way back to the eye of the knowledge gap tornado!

Therefore, at this stage, the organization must be very keen in avoiding repeated mistakes, and concentrate on getting ready, shielded from potential loss of knowledge, in case of losing a key professional or group.

### Preventing the Loss of Knowledge

Departing employees leave with more than what they know; they also take with them critical knowledge about who they know. That information needs to be a part of any knowledge-retention strategy. At this stage, the learning organization has shifted from an adaptive learning to a generative learning mode. It is now thinking proactively, instead of reactively. The goal here is to proactively shield itself from loss of knowledge, which would bring the organization back to a repeated mistake, a previous stage.

At this point an organization should not only be ready to prevent the loss of knowledge but also to turn learning into action.

### Turning Learning into Action

This is the final stage of the knowledge gap tornado before the organization restarts the process again, now in an outer ring around the tornado. If successful, the learning organization will be able to not only turn learning into action, which will tangibly and measurably impact the organization and the business bottom line, but the company will also receive a sort of reward, by acquiring silos of knowledge developed during its growth and transformation into a learning organization.

These silos of information, as long as they are interconnected and knowledge is shared, are very important in fueling the next cycle of growth of the company, making it knowledgeably stronger, more competitive and united on all fronts. At this stage the company breaks free from the stronger centrifugal forces of the tornado, as it distances itself from the eye. In addition, the company has business and learning momentum in its favor.

As with all the other stages, if the learning organization is not able to turn learning into action, chances are it is leaking knowledge somewhere, or it has lost knowledge in the process, either through the departure of a key professional, where knowledge had not been institutionalized, or by a failure in the institutionalization of knowledge within the organization.

# Identifying and Transferring Knowledge

Let's take as an example the World Bank Group, which has been dispensing loans to developing countries for more than 50 years. Owned by 185 member countries, the World Bank has about 10,000 employees—7,000 of them in the organization's headquarters, the remainder in field offices in 80 member countries. It also retains thousands of consultants; many of them retired bank officials. The Bank Group, which includes the IBRD and IDA as well as other affiliated entities such as the IFC, loans out about $20 billion annually, making it one of the world's largest sources of development assistance. The Bank had decided, back in 1996 that it would strive to become a knowledge bank. Since then, a variety of initiatives appeared that penetrated almost every corner of the organization, which indeed included the IT-like usual knowledge repositories and benchmarking efforts with other companies and consulting, but it transcended that.

In 2002, the bank began soliciting RFPs for a solution that would enable it to better organize and retrieve the millions of documents, many of them going back almost 60 years and written in dozens of languages, stored within its global repository. In effect, this would serve as the business intelligence solution for the bank's global knowledge sharing system. The vendor chosen—Teragram, a multilingual, natural-language technology company based in Cambridge, MA—makes categorization software that is used in high-demand environments such as large Internet search engines (Yahoo), major news companies (*The New York Times*), and numerous Fortune 500 companies and financial organizations. The bank chose Teragram's TK240 Version 5, the company's flagship taxonomy management software (software that automatically analyzes document contents and classifies and categorizes them). Typically, bank employees transmit documents to a document management system that uses the Oracle database. Each of these documents is read by the TK240 software, which applies linguistic-based identification to each document and then assigns meta-data tags based on predetermined indicators.

Web technology, which the bank characterizes as "the interface of choice for knowledge sharing," was also critical. Beginning in 2003, the bank began what it called the Internet Services Program (ISP), a multi-year project to upgrade its Internet capacities. To support this, it acquired IBM WebSphere Servers and WebSphere Portal Servers; Netegrity Web security software; iPlanet Directory Server; and Vignette content management software.

Today, World Bank's knowledge sharing has been mainstreamed into the organization, into regions and networks. There is more than 400 staff with the words "KM" in their titles. Also, certain key aspects of knowledge sharing such as Web, video databases, and portals have been accepted by nearly everyone. What the bank has that few other organizations can boast is integration with the organization's basic mission and processes, they have been able to identify, capture, and transfer learn into action.

Staples, in Framingham, MA, several years ago invested in KM in the hopes of encouraging their technical support employees spread in nine different locations, to share their technical know-how and best practices. Today, the results of the initiative have been very positive, resulted in shorter training sessions for Staples employees and faster response times by support personnel to customers.

### Gathering Knowledge

As discussed earlier in this book, one of the major mistakes KM professionals make is to rely on technology to deliver KM successfully. Technology, in particular KM software, should never dictate a KM strategy, nor hold back its implementation. Just as using Microsoft Word does not make its users better writers, buying IT implementations does not necessarily guarantee an organization's ability to identify, capture and transfer knowledge, in particular, into action.

Harder than dealing with the technology is getting people to accept and effectively utilize KM, as most often it will require changing their work habits and attitudes, which typically is not an easy task, as employees are never excited about sharing all they struggled to learn. That's why one of the biggest challenges to successfully implementing KM is to appropriately address the cultural change issues. The hype behind KM may wax and wane, but the business transformations under way in many private and public companies are true indications of the long-term value of knowledge and its management.

### Capturing Learning

Learning will always occur inside organizations, but in an unstructured fashion, more as a result of a benign neglect than deliberate and active support. This is so because knowledge workers and KM professionals want to invest in learning, but do not want to invest in nonproductive time. Unfortunately, organizational learning is still being viewed more as an academic training, even philosophical, and therefore, inefficient practice, than a strategy that can directly affect businesses' bottom line.

At the heart of organizational learning you should be able to find a series of processes that can be designed to capture, deploy, and lead. In other words, organizational learning encompasses a process of detection and correction of errors, as organizations learn through individuals, acting as agents, but prone to mistakes. The massive transformation in our business world is impacting every organization in the world, requiring each to renew and grow, and learning strategies might be the only alternative to sustain such a level of transformation (innovation) and growth.

### Learning in Action

While learning does not need to be conscious or intentional, it does not necessarily increase the learner's effectiveness. In addition, if the process of learning cannot be measured, such as, for example, by promoting observable changes in behavior throughout the organization, such effort would have failed. This is actually the typical situation organizations find themselves in: they are able to acquire the necessary know-how (the acquisition of knowledge) but have trouble mastering how to deploy, distribute, and implement the measures that will promote changed behavior within the organization.

At the heart of organizational learning lies a set of processes that can be designed, deployed, and led. We must identify the basic steps in every learning process, namely acquiring, interpreting, and applying knowledge, and then examine the critical challenges we face at each of these stages and the various ways the challenges. KM professionals should keep in mind that for learning organizations to succeed, four constructs must be integrally linked in the learning process of an organization: the acquisition of knowledge, the distribution of information, information interpretation, and organizational memory. In theory, the defining property of organization learning is the combination of same stimulus and different responses.

However it is quite rare to find such scenario in organizations, which makes me believe that either organizations don't learn in a consistent way, or that organizations learn but in nontraditional ways. Some may argue that organizations are not built to learn, but if you agree that organizations are not the buildings and the processes they sustain, but the people, the professionals, that are part of them, then organizational learning involves a different kind of learning than has been described in most literature available.

## Adaptive Learning Versus Generative Learning

When it comes to learning, a characteristic of corporate business operations is always based upon coping with challenges that rise every day and adapting to them as required. This type of adaptive learning trend is actually a starting point, but as Peter Senge points out in his book *The Fifth Discipline*, not only is this increasing adaptiveness a first stage in the process, but there is also a tremendous need for companies to focus on a generative learning, also known as double-loop learning.

An adaptive learning organization only focuses on solving current problems without examining the appropriateness of actual learning behaviors. It only focuses on incremental improvements, often based upon the past track record of success. Thus, in such learning environment the fundamental assumptions underlying the existing ways of doing work are never questioned. The essential difference is between being adaptive and having adaptability.

Conversely, instead of reacting and adapting to new situations and challenges, generative learning organizations adopt a more proactive approach, as it emphasizes the continuous experimentation and feedback, always examining the way organizations define and solve problems. Thus, I believe, a very innovative role of knowledge workers today is to promote generative learning within the organization. Knowledge workers are the right professionals for the job because generative learning is all about creating alternatives, creating new paradigms. It requires a systemic thinking that encompasses business process and human behavior in organizations, cultural stereotypes, keen vision and above all, strategic thinking. Further, knowledge workers must ensure the sharing of visions and remember that success is the equivalent of visions in action. A vision without action is the same as never waking up from a dream. By the same token, actions without a vision, is the same as sailing without a compass, without a destination.

Generative learning, aside from a shared vision, also requires a great amount of personal mastery. It goes on to include not only proficiency in its business trade, but also team learning, and creative tension, which is a very hard environment to create and stay in, as this situation is reflected between the vision and the current reality. By comparison, generative learning, unlike adaptive, pushes the envelope in the way Japanese companies typically attempt to accomplish the same thing with strategic and interpretive equivocality, as it requires new ways of looking at the world and reacting to it, not by adapting, but by interacting with it. That's the double loop.

## Identifying and Transferring Knowledge

Another major challenge surrounding knowledge workers today is motivating people to contribute and share their knowledge. Be it for lack of time to write something that can help someone else or simply uneasiness in sharing what they know, employees and other knowledge professionals are not readily willing to spend the time (and their knowledge). To tell them that knowledge sharing improves learning, which has direct impact on the business bottom line, does not always have a high rate of success. However, examples of successful learning organizations, such as IBM and Johnson & Johnson shows, almost at a truism level, that knowledge sharing pays off.

More than ever before, an organization's success will be measured by its level of adaptability and flexibility, not the usual short-term profitability and productivity indicators. These indicators are nothing more than a current snapshot of the company's success at that particular time, not the strength of its management and its ability to remain successful in the long run.

### Improving Collaboration

It is true that new ideas are essential if learning is to take place. But the fact that your organization generates an abundance of new ideas and these ideas are being turned into knowledge doesn't mean you have turned your organization into a learning one. That's because raw and unfiltered information often is of limited value. Knowledge workers must be skilled in giving meaning to the data they have collected and make sure this information is shared across the organization. Unless raw knowledge is interpreted, the information generated from it will remain unutilized. In addition, to improve knowledge interpretation and sharing organizations must get better at collaboration. Knowledge workers must simplify the process of sharing knowledge. If the value proposition of doing this is not made clear, it will not get done.

In his book *Simplicity, Speed and Self-Confidence: An Interview with Jack Welch*, Ram Charan[1] discusses GE's problem-solving process modeled after a New England town meeting. "Work-Out," as this process was called by Welch, had two main practical goals: an intellectual and a practical one. The practical was to get rid of bad habits accumulated since the establishment of GE. The intellectual one aimed at redefining the relationship between supervisors and subordinates, by putting these leaders in front of their own people several times a year to let them learn what and how their people think about the business, themselves and their leaders.

KM portals can also be used as an effective strategy to deliver customizable, multidimensional interface to enable searchable access to data and applications. These portals can include not only content management tools, such as search and retrieval, access to electronic news and information, as well as repository for documents, websites and databases, but also collaboration and group productivity tools.

## Chapter Summary

Chapter 3 is an important chapter, addressing strategies to turn corporate knowledge into action, into concrete project results. It discusses the need for organizations becoming learning organization, which in the process requires it to be open to dissonant information and conflicts, which ultimately can foster innovation. The chapter also addresses techniques in capturing, transferring, and disseminating knowledge by improving collaboration.

# CHAPTER 4

# Nurturing Learning Organizations

The transfer of knowledge within a learning organization is a complex task. However, taken seriously and with the support of senior management it can be accomplished. Not that I have met any learning organization in its full sense; I haven't and I don't think I ever will. But such generative learning condition is to be cultivated, even though you may never be able to become a true learning organization. Achieving such a level is like achieving the full sense of personal humility, or even Zen. Once you believe and affirm you have reached it, you would have just missed it.

To succeed in shaping your organization's future, you must develop an organization that learns well, efficiently and constantly. Such learning is critical, because competing in rapidly changing environments means your organization must be able to track your environments, identify changes, and adjust to these changes. You must try new things and determine what works and what does not work—increasing what does and swiftly abandoning that which does not. Then you must build a new cycle of learning upon this learning in a never-ending fashion.

Therefore, knowledge professionals and executive staff must be aware that if organizations are not able to cope with the rapidly changing business environment, which also encompasses technology and human behavior within the organization, it will die. I strongly believe that organizational learning will become as important to corporations as vitamins and minerals are to the human body: depleted of it, the whole system gradually breaks down and becomes ill, and if not replenished, it eventually succumbs.

According to Garratt (p. 67, 2000),[1] loops of learning (and transferring of learning, I might add) allow the critical review of all levels of the organization. Such continuous learning enables the organization to sense and respond to the changes in its external and internal environments to ensure the survival and development of the energy niches that support it. This is a very holistic approach, much like nurturing a living organism, as most of the learning and transferring of it inside the organization is personal, private, very often uncodified, hidden and, most of all, a defensive way of coping with the effects of a seemingly nonlearning employer.

## Effectively Transferring Knowledge

Why is knowledge transferring so important?, you might ask. Back in 1498, Wang Yang-Ming was already saying that "knowledge is the beginning of practice; doing is the completion of knowing."[2] The former Chairman of SAS Airlines, Jan Carlson, believes that "an individual without information cannot take responsibility; an individual who is given information cannot help but take responsibility."[3] The same is true for knowledge workers and their responsibility in bridging the knowledge gap inside the organization. A key strategy in this process is the effective transferring of knowledge.

To bridge this knowledge gap, knowledge workers must realize that the utmost knowledge base in any organization does not reside in computer databases, but in the heads of the individuals inside the organization. The majority of professionals inside knowledge-based organizations worldwide have college degrees. Many of them hold postgraduate degrees and a large amount of know-how based on previous experiences and specializations. The challenge is, how do you get each one of these professionals to share what they know, not compulsorily, but freely and openly with everyone else in the organization? In addition, how do you get them to accept responsibility for their actions? Where should your focus and line of actions be? In my experience, it has to cover a multitude of areas, including:

- identifying target individuals;
- knowing the barriers in the organization;
- having a code of ethics;
- fostering culture change;
- promoting Innovation by thinking out of the box.

## Identifying Target Individuals

For any successful knowledge transfer activity, it is important for you to identify the individuals from whom you need capital knowledge transferred. Unfortunately, I find that the more important the transfer of knowledge is, and the capturing for that matter, the more difficult it is to identify and locate these professionals, never mind get them to share what they learn or know. Take for instance the global consulting companies. To locate their professionals can be hard at times. Often, if you were to weigh the average amount of time professional consultants spend between offices across the country and the globe, at any point in time, you may find that 86% of them will be outside the office and many times outside of the country.

In an organization where the office is not the place where business is conducted, knowledge transfer can be a very hard job to accomplish. The same is true for any other organization, maybe not at such high levels as in the professional consulting industry. For instance, if I am in my office for 40 h a week, then my time in the office is less than 25% of my available time. If I consider the times I am working from home or a hotel room, then the percentage falls even more. Among the big six consulting firms, you may find that their consultants are in the office less than 14 percent of their available time.

Therefore, knowing where your people are and how they will contribute to the transfer of knowledge is very important, and must be taken into consideration before you establish a collaboration strategy.

## Identifying Organizational Barriers

What are the barriers you are likely to face in attempting knowledge transfer implementation? These barriers are real, and they exist in every organization. A typical one is the structural barrier of hierarchical organizations, such as departments, groups and divisions. Different operating companies in different countries, language and cultural barriers are often present as well. There are many more barriers and you must take the time to identify them and have a strategy to overcome each one of them prior to any knowledge transferring initiative.

In order for any knowledge transfer initiative to be successful you must not focus your efforts on a department or an operating company, but on the total company, across all of these barriers. To do this you will have to focus on increasing the ability of the individual in communicating his thoughts to others in the organization, as it would be the collective result of a lot of individual actions that would be necessary to produce a result for the company. The question is how do you increase the power of these individuals sharing their thoughts with others in the organization?

There are many areas you should concentrate on in attempting to become a learning organization and striving to transfer knowledge at the same time. One of the main areas of attack should include increasing the power of individuals in sharing their thoughts and overcoming the organization's barriers.

### Encouraging Culture Change

Board of directors and executive staff are responsible for the climate they create in the organization. Such climate has a major impact on the organization's ability to share knowledge across time and space. Over the years I have seen this as the most difficult aspect of knowledge transfer. By default, people have always taught themselves to collect knowledge over the years as a way to achieve power, or as a way of professional self-preservation, to say the least. What is thought in colleges and universities is that knowledge should be acquired and used, but we never learned how to share it.

Another important aspect to consider is with regard to the quality of the people that you, as a learning organization, can bring to this relationship with partners, supply chain, and distribution channels, which will determine the level at which your organization can operate in this relationship. The higher the quality of the individuals engaged in this knowledge transfer, the higher the quality of the knowledge that can be brought to bear on any problem that your customers and co-workers bring to you. But don't underestimate other levels of the organization, as every individual, independent of their role, can effectively contribute to this KM initiative. At Buckman, their goal was to have 80 percent of their organization effectively engaged on the front line by the end of 2000.

Such level of knowledge sharing/transferring assumes different shapes according to the organization in which it is implemented. It may translate, as in Buckman's case, in how do they get as many people as possible creating and transferring as much knowledge as possible in the best way possible in order to have a positive impact on the customer. Some organizations may focus on making sure that there is a high level of interaction between the organization's people and paying customers for a measurable frequency and duration. For others, it might be to ensure that the majority of their people actively use their electronic forums, web portals and e-mail, or even to ensure that they get their accounting right, which may include profit recovery activities, so that their groups measure up to this new corporate goal.

My advice is, no matter what the nuances, idiosyncrasies, and specifics of any given learning organization, the goal of knowledge transferring strategies is to bring about the full weight of the knowledge that exists in the hardware, software, and people, in a relevant and useful manner, to bear upon the requirements of the customer. I believe that any learning organization, especially those that realized they must adopt a generative learning attitude versus an adaptive attitude, is doing a lot of these things already. But if they can get all of their people exercising knowledge transfer at all times, a tremendous power can be unleashed. The goal here is not to go after definitions, numbers, procedures, or any other quantifiable business goals. It should be about involvement, commitment, creativity, passion, and ultimately the freedom to do everything the organization can, and to use all of the knowledge it has, to make sure that it has done its best to satisfy customers—inside and outside the organization—in all areas.

Knowledge transferring will only be successful when you are able to fully and effectively engage all of your people, with a technological system and within cultural surroundings where they can all be comfortable practicing it. Only then will you have sufficiently addressed the collaboration and knowledge transferring issues of your organization.

## KM Strategies to Foster Knowledge Transfer

As discussed earlier, learning must be turned into action in order to be effective. A learning organization is a breathing organism, and if it is not flourishing, it is dying. Value and use the knowledge of the organization on the job, turn learning into action, and achieve KM performance. You might be in for a surprise here, but do the people in your organization know how to create value and make money for the company? If so, do they know what kind of knowledge they need to accomplish this?

Just as any professional sports team, players have their strengths and their weaknesses. They perform better in one position rather than others. As part of becoming a learning organization, you might have to deal with miscast positions, as well as not-so-fit ones. The way employees deal with knowledge, and the positions they hold, can mean the difference between your organization's success and failure. Thus, be prepared to conduct some knowledge performance targets to match.

Therefore, building a KM strategy is often the best starting point when attempting to implement knowledge transfer strategy. The implementation will require you to know and understand what knowledge and systems the organization needs to enhance for its competitive advantage. There are four key components in KM you must address: KM applications, intuitive content management, KM culture, KM-based governance.

## Augmenting Knowledge Sharing Proficiencies

For a learning organization to foster knowledge sharing it must become proficient in collaboration. To do that the organization must be able to shift from a culture where hoarding knowledge is power, to one where sharing knowledge is power. This is not an easy task, as individuals are the ones holding the knowledge and most often they feel very insecure about sharing knowledge, becoming obsolete for the organization and losing value, which then generates the fear of being let go.

Therefore, the main challenge here for KM professionals is to get people to share what they know. Sharing is the basis of collaboration among people and any learning organization. Curiously, people across the organization often do not know what it means to share and use knowledge. So, knowledge workers must educate, empower the organization to understand such collaboration concept, and get them going. Therefore, it becomes imperative that a dedicated team is created, with special skill sets, to act as knowledge brokers inside the organization.

The following strategies of collaboration offer different benefits to a learning organization. Beware, these models require special manners and measures of organizational support, and the more models an organization adopts, the greater are its chances of becoming a successful learning organization:

- Meeting and Working the Network of Collaboration—This collaboration strategy usually commences with a face-to-face meeting, a strategy or brainstorm meeting, a business or social gathering, or even a telephone call or e-mail exchange. Two people meet, identify some synergies, identify value in each other, and then resolve to keep in touch. Although collaboration at this stage doesn't yet exist, it has a lot of potential. If the strategy is successful, over time these two people will trade stories and backgrounds, compare acquaintances, and unearth each other's skills, interests, and areas of expertise. Furthermore, they might build trust and rapport, even though they may not even, at that stage, have any interest in helping one another. But they remain open to the possibilities that may arise to possibly working together on a project, or have a chance to share some valuable knowledge. Such a process is far beyond the organization's control, as at this level, the process is still highly personal and often arises through serendipity (God set the times and the places!). This personal collaboration strategy requires very little technology beyond basic communications, is often unplanned, and little support beyond providing opportunities for exposure to others is necessary. Executive education courses, seminars, symposia, trade associations, service organizations, charities, on-line discussion groups, book signings—indeed, any forum where interesting people congregate—provide rich environments for creating relationships.

- User Groups and Task Forces: A Need for Collaboration— Collaboration here is premeditated, as there was a need to focus on a very particular subject or object. Typically, this type of collaboration assumes the form of user groups, focus groups, task forces and so on, because a group or individual lacks all the skills or resources necessary to accomplish the desired outcome. For instance, President Reagan appointed a panel to investigate the explosion of the space shuttle Challenger. One panelist, Dr. Richard Feynman, used a cup of ice water and a strip of rubber to demonstrate that the explosion occurred because a rubber O-ring had failed at low temperature. But Feynman only got the idea to consider temperature because Donald Kutyna, an Air Force general on the investigative panel with him, remarked to Feynman that while working on his car, he had wondered about the effects of temperature on rubber. Just by asking questions you can promote collaboration. Bringing together communities of practice is also a more elaborate way to promote collaboration. This strategy builds on the serendipitous nature of the first (i.e., "I know a guru who can help us with that issue!"). But for active collaboration to start, or for such teams to form, people have to be able to find each other, and the life of these collaborating teams may extend beyond the current need, but it is more likely that they will evolve or dissolve as needs change.

Generation of ideas should be fostered in every learning organization. Translating great ideas into new contexts can save the organization time and money, while raising the average level of outcome quality and implementation. Of course, you may decide to modify previous inventions as they change environments, but that is OK. Velcro, for instance, has continually tailored its original product to include new resins with unique properties for specialized applications, inexpensive disposable closures for diapers and heavy-use closures like those on a blood pressure cuff.

The major requirement when transferring knowledge is to have a robust corporate memory, with a KM gathering and collaboration system for users to contribute or review ideas, experiences and work solutions, as well as to access the contributions, searching both broadly across disciplines. Web portals are particularly suited to supporting such contribution and retrieval and for enabling unexpected connections and discoveries.

## Chapter Summary

This chapter emphasized the importance of nurturing learning organizations in effectively transfer knowledge among its staff and leadership. The chapter assists in developing strategies to identify targeting individuals to aid in the dissemination of knowledge and to deal with organizational barriers against the culture of change.

# CHAPTER 5

# Knowledge Technologies

A lot has been discussed about the limitations of an adaptive learning organization and a generative one. We live in a world of rapid changes, economic and technological, as well as cultural and political. In order to remain competitive, organizations must be able to transform, both to adapt to the changed business environment, as well as to proactively ready themselves for the next wave of changes to come.

Transformation, in turn, requires excellence in strategy, organization, and systems. When all these three components are effectively considered, not only can the implementation risks associated with any transformation within an organization be reduced, but also success can readily be achieved. After all, the goal of knowledge workers and knowledge managers is to ensure every individual in the organization is ready for transformations at any given time.

The ultimate goal of KM is to enable the development of collaborative enterprise systems that allow every individual inside the organization to become a learner, as according to Hoffman,[1] "learners, in a world of change, inherit the world, [while] learned remains beautifully equipped to deal with a world that does not exist." Knowledge workers can tremendously increase an organization's effectiveness through common knowledge practices. Knowledge is the key differentiator in today's business, and the one responsible for all the business transformation that is taking place. So, you either lead it or follow.

Now, capitalizing on knowledge is actually not as complex as managing it. When it comes to running a business successfully, the greatest CEOs rely on common sense, not complex mathematical formulas. As Ram Charan[2] describes, it is necessary business acumen. I believe, as part of this business acumen, knowledge workers should help CEOs and the executive staff to also understand how to build enterprise systems, to deal with the peril, promises, and the future. After all, information must be managed.

## Organizing Knowledge and Know-How Through Business Thinking Practices

Organizing knowledge and know-how requires interdisciplinary and multidisciplinary skills. Having a great focused knowledge on a particular segment of the company or industry will not suffice. On the contrary, it will create barriers to full understanding of business and common sense across the organization. That's why I keep emphasizing the role of knowledge workers in developing business thinking practices that not only the executive staff can tap in to, but also the whole organization. Any learning organization must understand the total business cycle every business abides by in order to be able to measure quantifiable business results, as depicted in Figure 5.1

As we learn to view a learning organization as a whole, not broken into departments, functions, or tasks, it will begin to function in a more fluid way. Meetings will be less bureaucratic and more goals oriented. The organization will also be more transparent between distinct groups and the total business cycles phases.

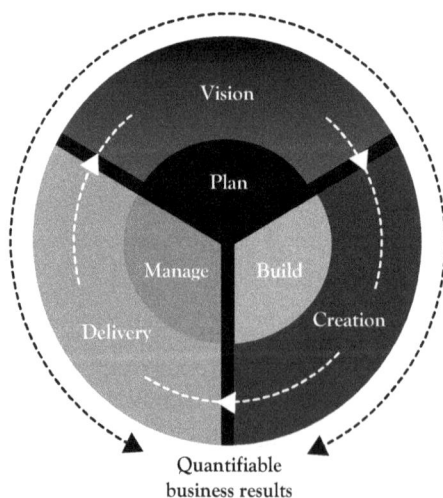

*Figure 5.1. Understanding the main elements of a total business cycle is important in developing business thinking practices.*

## At the Core of Every Business Thinking Practice

At the core of every business thinking practice you will find the same: the goal is to make a profit. To make money a business needs to generate cash, and add that to return on assets (ROA) and to growth. Now, how do you get the whole organization to think that way? By being their best coach.

The difference between an organization and a football team is that the organization has to deal with very tangible milestones (well, the team must score!) and needs to produce quarterly reports. In both instances, to be successful, you still have to develop a knowledge strategy, one that organizes knowledge and know-how, and then enables it to be shared throughout the organization and among its business partners.

To seek competitive advantage you must be convinced that the organization's knowledge needs to be organized and managed more effectively, being readily available to be exploited in the marketplace. Knowledge and know-how, as well as other forms of intellectual capital, are your company's hidden assets. Although they are not visible in quarterly reports and annual report balance sheets, they underline the creation of value and future earnings potential. That is why knowledge intensive companies such as Apple, Facebook, Microsoft, Roche, and Glaxo Wellcome have market values at least 10 times the value of their physical assets.

## Thinking Practices Generating Knowledge Advantage

One of the main thinking practices in KM is to realize how organizations can use knowledge to secure a strategic advantage. Basically, it is by generating greater value through the knowledge, thus acquiring know-how in products, people and processes, for instance:

- People's Know-how: Anglian Water, one of the leading providers of water and wastewater services in the United Kingdom, has been investing in learning organization programs as one way of nurturing and applying underutilized talent within the company.
- Processes' Know-how: Texas Instruments realized that it was typical to often find differences in performance levels of 3:1

or more among different groups performing the same process. They decided to invest in KM applied to their processes to close the knowledge gap, which saved the company the cost of one new semiconductor fabrication plant, or $1 billion in investments, if you prefer.

- Products' Know-how: Petrobras, the Brazilian petroleum company, one of the largest in the world, realized that intelligent products could promote premium prices and be more beneficial to users, so they invested in an intelligent oil drilling system that bends, and weaved its way to extract more oil than ever from the pockets of oil under oceanic ground formations.

Such examples of strategic advantage developed through KM are only one way that investing in knowledge pays off. Another is through active management of intellectual property (IP) portfolio of patents and licenses, as well as organizing knowledge so you can exploit it internally by generating information and know-how.

### *Promoting Team Work as Knowledge Transfer Tool*

If we take the example of a cardiac surgery team, we find this is a team that must work very closely together. In an operating room, a patient is rendered functionally dead while a knowledgeable surgical team conducts the surgery. The amount of synchronized knowledge transfer, in real time, and teamwork that goes on is just astonishing. Any mistakes can be disastrous.

The most interesting thing is that such teams are not that different from your executive staff or any other cross-functional team so crucial to business success. Learning organizations can learn a lot from such high-risk surgical teams, in particular with regard to executing existing processes efficiently, and most important, by implementing new processes as quickly as possible.

In the process of becoming an effective learning organization you will have to adopt new technologies and very likely new business processes, which is a highly disruptive task. In addition, you will have to focus on how your organization's teams learn and why some learn faster than others. To be successful, organizations must capitalize on leaders that actively manage their group's learning efforts. And when implementing new technologies and processes, make sure these innovations are directly targeted at learning; every individual in the team is highly motivated to learn and upper management is fostering an environment of psychological safety through effective communication and innovation.

Of course, to convince traditional organizations that teams learn more efficiently if they are explicitly managed for learning poses a challenge in many areas of business. One of the main challenges is that the majority of team leaders are chosen not for their management skills, but for their technical expertise. Thus, to be successful, organizations must invest in team leaders that are adept at creating learning environments. Upper management must be able to look beyond technical competencies and work with leaders who can motivate and manage teams of disparate specialists.

Using teamwork as a knowledge transfer tool enables you to tap into not only the explicit knowledge of team members, but also tacit ones. The goal should be adopt a new sense-and-respond business model that can help the organization anticipate, adapt and respond to continually changing business needs. Team members should be able to identify the three main stages of learning and strive to close the circle of learning, as depicted in Figure 5.2. Stages of learning: by identifying, striving and closing the learning stages circle members of a learning organization can be better equipped to sense-and-respond to new business needs.

In order for teamwork to be effective, it must be able to generate and share new knowledge. As Figure 5.2 shows, there are three learning stages any individual or team must go through to successfully learn, deploy, and share new acquired knowledge.

The first stage, the acquisition of information, raw materials of learning is gathered. It is very important for those in this stage *to know what they want to know, from where, and for what purpose.* Otherwise, not only will they end up with an information overflow, but they will also know a lot of irrelevant stuff—useless knowledge. As discussed in

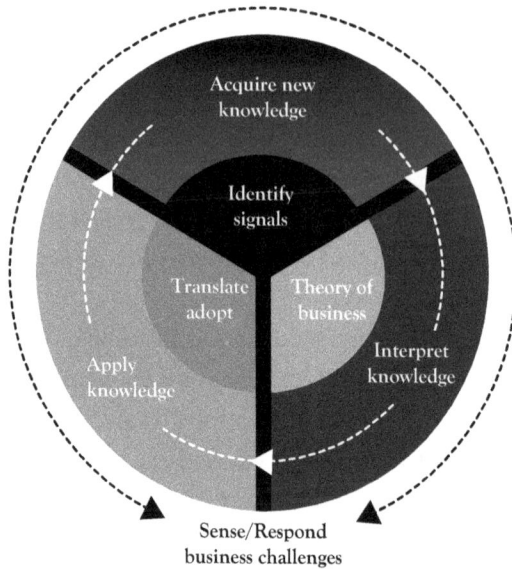

*Figure 5.2. Stages of learning: by identifying, striving, and closing the learning stages circle members of a learning organization can be better equipped to sense-and-respond to new business needs.*

chapter one, Sir Francis Bacon's premise that *knowledge is* power no longer holds true if knowledge is not followed by action, a successful and purposeful one.

The second stage, the interpretation of information, requires the development of perspectives, positions, opinions, and elaborated understanding. At this level, materials collected in the first stage are analyzed and reviewed. Here, you must make sure that there is an understanding about what that information means, and the cause-and-effect of the relationships it produces once applied.

The last stage, the application of information, is when organizations finally decide to engage in tasks, activities, and very important, new behavior. It is here that analyses are translated into action. It is here that the organization must ask itself what new activities are appropriate or necessary. What behaviors must be modified? David Garvin wrote extensively about the process of turning learning into action in his book *Learning in Action*,[3] which I strongly recommend if you really want to put your learning organization to work. Another excellent book, and more recent, is *Know Can Do!: How to Put Learning Into Action*, by Blanchard, Meyer, and Ruhe, published by Macmillan in 2007.

## Adapting to Unpredictable Demands

Organizations will be able to adapt in a systematic way to the unpredictable demands of rapid and relentless changes if they are designed and managed as an adaptive system. However, even though adaptive strategies are very important in the face of change, the ultimate goal of any learning organization is to be able to predict the changes before they occur and position themselves proactively, instead of reactively. The questions knowledge managers and executive staff should be asking at all times is: first, how can they integrate the organization, as a whole, to achieve its business purposes; and second, how can they cope with the rate of changes inside and outside the organization, and still be able to create an organization's "central brain" that keeps the rate of change of the organization equal to or greater than the rate of environmental chance.

Bill Gates, in his now old (yet current!) but still legendary book *Business @ the Speed of Thought*,[4] alluded to the importance of an organization's digital nervous system. Enterprise systems can enormously help organizations to think rationally about developing this much needed digital nervous system, as it presents a new model of corporate computing. Although knowledge workers may not have the power of implementing such systems, which legally comes from above, from the Board, the key idea here is to tap continuously into the natural daily learning of every individual in the organization.

Browne, in his book *Unleashing the Power of Learning*,[5] comments on BP Amoco as one of the most serious implementers of digital nervous systems, because of their focus on continuous learning across the organization and its hierarch. Enterprise system implementations must take into consideration both micro- and macro-political levels. The micro-political level or internal world of the organization deals with the energies and blockages generated by the existing organization's capabilities. The macro-political level, or the world outside the organization, deals with the changes in the political, economic, social, technological, and physical environment trends, in an attempt to increase the organization's effectiveness.

The enterprise system also allows companies to replace their existing information systems, which are often incompatible with one another, with a single, integrated system. The object is to streamline data flows throughout an organization. Software packages, such as those offered by ORACLE, SAP, and IFS, can dramatically improve an organization's efficiency and bottom line. But despite the many advantages these system provide, you must be careful with the risks they bring, in particular their ability to tie your hands!

Therefore, be it because you need to assess your organization's capabilities or the enterprise system, make sure to assess the pros and cons of implementing the system very carefully, as any new system introduced can produce unintended and highly disruptive results. Many companies incur huge losses more often than they should when entering uncharted waters, such as new alliances and partnerships, new markets, products or technologies. Often, many of these failures could have been prevented if upper management had approached innovative ventures with the right plan and control tools. Both the board members and executive staff should always be ready to fight the techno-babble of functional specialists, and so the ability to make wise decisions is much improved by the collective critical debate. Discovery-driven planning is also a practical tool to be used at such times, as it acknowledges the difference between planning for a new venture and for a more conventional business. Often, the organization may have to evaluate the bottom line and work its way up the income statement first, before determining the need for a new venture's profit potential.

To comply with such action learning process, I believe Figure 5.2 must be modified to provide some "circuit breakers" that would flag learning situations that may lead to pernicious actions for the organization and business as a whole. My model is based on Garvin's model, as he discusses it in *Learning in Action*. However, I borrow from Garratt's concept of an action learning cycle as well, as he discusses it in The Learning Organization: Developing Democracy at Work, to only expand these models to provide validation in every step. Figure 5.3 depicts my view of an action learning cycle for the 21st century learning organization, where

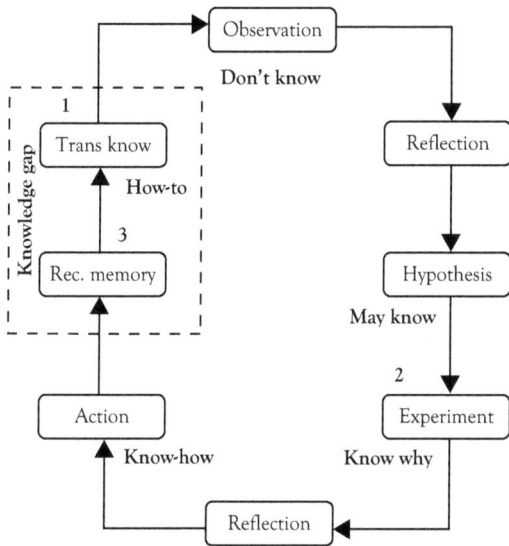

*Figure 5.3. The action learning cycle for the 21st century organizations.*

time is an asset, mistakes are almost unforgiving, and the inability of an organization to adapt to new environments is synonyms with slow death, as organizations must strive to obsolete themselves every day before the market does it for them.

As Figure 5.3 shows, the design of an action learning process is based on simplicity. And simplicity should be viewed as understanding the whole. It should generate excitement, should be easy to view and should be timeless. The role of knowledge workers is to help organizations to go through change. Once upper management, the executive staff, figures out a strategy, the knowledge worker's job should be to help translate it to the rest of the organization that has to do the work. Building trust and competence for this to become an organizational way of life is not a quick task, and tends to be complex. Pilot actions learning process might be appropriate, followed by public evaluation, so you can build trust, while at the same time, through learning, you build values and behaviors that are rewarded, so that they become part of the organization's culture.

From this reflective process, depicted in Figure 5.3, learning organizations can break away from the action-fixated cycle of nonlearning, which so bedevils many organizations throughout the world. Typically, individuals tend to avoid a reflective approach to their work and end up jumping into inconsequent and fruitless actions because they already have a hard time just figuring out what they are supposed to do. The 21st century economy, with its reengineering and total quality management (TQM) strategies, with its more leaning approach, has streamlined task work, but knowledge work has become even more cluttered and confusing than ever before. Thus, making fast and right choices, while the economy changes before our eyes every second, is now the toughest part of getting any work done.

In Figure 5.3, projects are integrated into an organization-wide, action learning-base transformation process. This enables learning to be continuously available from each project, but also the organization can see more easily the patterns arising from that learning. The main differentiator in the paradigm I propose is that:

- In the first stage of the learning cycle, the *observation stage*, individuals should feel comfortable to be in a position of *not knowing*, so they can actually observe new learning patterns. Pride, ego, seniority aspects, and corporate hierarchy should all be left aside.

- In the second stage, *reflection*, any new information acquired must pass through a filter of reflection. This is necessary not only to evaluate the relevance of such information, but also to determine how practical, how applicable, such information is for the task at hand or future tasks. In the 21st century economy, there is no power or sense in becoming a human *Encyclopedia Britannica*, as the most important aspect is to be able to turn knowledge into action, to be able to cope with the change of environments and, ideally, anticipate changes to come.

- In the third stage, *hypothesis*, individuals should be able to reach a point where they have acquired enough information to formulate a hypothesis. They should be able to have an idea of what they learned, of what they now *may know*. When testing hypothesis, keep it deductive, rather than inductive, disciplined, rather than playful, and targeted rather than open-ended. The goal here should be to prove, to prepare material for validation during the next stage, experimentation. As pointed out by Lawler,[6] managers tend to fail here because they believe they are failing to mesh with the realities of life in their organizations. This is very important so they can go to the experimental stage with a clear focus of what needs to be tested, and what needs to be validated. The question is: what do they think they know? What do they think they are learning?

- In the fourth stage, *experimentation*, the goal is to achieve a level where you know-why. To learn new information just because doesn't make sense. With all that has changed in how we work, we need to work smarter, instead of harder and faster. Thus it is important for the learning process that individuals know what they need to learn, what they think they are learning, and why the information is what it is. They must experiment with the new information, they must try it out, so they can trust it, and value can be added to their skills set. Keep in mind that for experiments to be successful, the focus must shift from justification and commitment to skepticism and doubt. Knowledge here should be regarded as provisional, and conclusions as tentative. Otherwise, prevailing views will not be subjected to testing, and experimentation will exist only in name. The same applies to ambiguity, as the higher it is, less objective are the insights taken from the experiment. Notice in Figure 5.3 that experimentation is the second step (number 2) in bridging the knowledge gap in the organization, as individuals are only able to share knowledge they can experiment.

- In the fifth stage, *reflection*, a first revolution of learning is concluded, as individuals come full circle with the learning process. At this stage they should be able to look back on what they did not know, reflect on what they needed to know, and how they came to formulate a hypothesis about what they may get to know and the results of the experimentation they undertook. Reviews and reflections must be conducted immediately, while the experience and memory is still fresh and data can be validated. Thus, at this stage the new information should have been validated, and a plan to action using this new information should be at work. Otherwise, the process should start again, back to observation.

- In the sixth stage, *action*, individuals must be able to turn learning into action, to turn know-why into know-how. In the stage before (reflection), the primary problem is passivity, an inability or unwillingness to act on new interpretations. Many times individuals will resist new information and rather restart the learning process, back into observation, as they feel that this information *can't be right*. That's why experimentation is important, but still, people tend to disregard hard facts, when such information means a behavioral change and most people are risk-averse. As Jack Welch of General Electric stated in his book *Jack: Straight from the Gut*, "change has no constituency."[7] Therefore, to turn leaning into action, a certain level of self-awareness is essential. The results of the experimentation stage, the current practices, must be understood, so action can take place.

- In the seventh stage, *recording in the memory* (corporate memory), individuals should record their newly acquired know-how, or know-how they learned they already had, in the corporation's memory bank. This stage is also very important, and its absence or underutilization is partially responsible for what I call knowledge gap. That is what the small number 3 next to the box signifies, as recording and sharing the knowledge they have is vital for knowledge transfer and management, and without it, there is no learning organization. Arnold Kransdorff's books, *Corporate Amnesia*[8] and *Knowledge Management: Begging for a Bigger Role*,[9] describe many organizations failing to codify and distribute their learning due to a lack of structured corporate memory, the digital nervous system Gates talks about. Without such recording practices, organizations will learn nothing, and forget nothing as well. Such organizations have not learned that history repeats itself, but first as tragedy, then as farce! This stage emphasizes the vital importance of KM implementations and enterprise systems.

- The eighth stage, *knowledge transfer*, is the final in the learning cycle, but the most important in bridging the knowledge gap within organizations. It's actually the first step (small number 1 in Figure 5.3), when knowledge is finally institutionalized within the organization. Unfortunately, not many companies take the time to reflect on their experiences and develop lessons for the future. KM professionals and managers in general must help individuals and work teams carefully review the new information learned and distinguish effective from ineffective practice, and also, in stage seven, must record their findings in an accessible form, and in stage eight, disseminate the results to the other individuals in the organization.

Lastly, ask yourself what strategies your organization is adopting to maximize the returns on your knowledge asset. Try to make better use of the knowledge that already exists within your organization by utilizing the action learning cycle discussed above. In my experience, I've heard several KM professionals and group leaders lamenting that *if only they knew what they knew*. It's common to find individuals in one department or group in the organization reinventing the wheel or failing to solve customers' problems just because the knowledge they need is elsewhere in the company but not known or accessible to them. Hence, knowledge workers and KM professionals typically focus first on installing or improving an Intranet.

Also consider focusing on innovation as well, the creation of new knowledge and turning ideas into valuable products and services. This is sometimes referred to as knowledge innovation. Don't confuse it with R&D or creativity though. There is plenty of creativity in organizations; you just need to make sure you don't lose it, and allow it to flow throughout the organization and find its way to where it can be used. To do that you will need to invest in better innovation, knowledge conversion and transfer, and eventually commercialization processes. This thrust of strategy is the most difficult, yet ultimately has the best potential for improved company performance.

## Chapter Summary

This chapter provided an overview of knowledge technologies concepts and its use in organizing knowledge and know-how through business thinking practices. The chapter also discussed the promotion of teamwork as a knowledge transfer tool.

# CHAPTER 6

# Having a Mindset of Knowledge Capital

As Paul Strassmann[1] points out, companies should be focusing on identifying and increasing the level of what he calls "information productivity," which he considers a key index of a company's strength or weakness. According to Strassmann, senior management should be measuring the value added by information

[Net Profit – (Financial Capital Assets × Interest Rate for Borrowing)/ Cost of Information Management or Cost of Sales, General & Administrative + Cost of R&D]

Unfortunately, more companies are destroying knowledge assets than actively generating them. The problem is that our narrow-minded dependence on traditional accounting principles has failed to account for knowledge in any meaningful way, becoming one of the key reasons for the corporate world's continuing troubles. By contrast, companies such as Apple, eBay, HP, Microsoft, Abbott Laboratories, and Coca-Cola have long ago grasped the vital importance of valuing and managing knowledge, and therefore have taken their industries by storm.

I contend that the inability of many U.S. and international companies to turn their know-how into effective action items is responsible for pushing information productivity to negative level. As argued by Strassmann, information is being treated as an instantly perishable commodity. Unfortunately, organizations are failing to recognize and measure the contributions of people to the generation of information and knowledge. None of these contributions to creating greater economic value are being recognized.

Furthermore, if you take a look at the annual costs of information, you will realize that they have long ago surpassed the costs of equity capital; except for some organizations, such as in mining, steel, transportation and real estate, the scarce commodity is information. Nonetheless, it is through effective information management practices that the users of information are able to create all business value.

One of the main challenges in the process of capitalizing knowledge is finding out best practices for measuring and valuing knowledge assets. Actually this is an old challenge, being around for more than 20 years. The literature on the subject is vast, so it is the number of attempts. Tom Stewart,[2] back in 1991 makes intellectual capital the attribute of an organization. But it is Leif Edvinsson, Skandia, and Pat Sullivan who brought a more pragmatic definition to intellectual capital, as knowledge that can be converted into value.[3]

Unless professionals can transform know-how into how-to, theory into practice, tacit knowledge into explicit, they not only would have failed in the transference of knowledge, but also would widen the knowledge gap within the organization. Again, I point out to Strassmann's excellent evaluation of the problem, as he conveys that the problem is that organizations are trying to work the problem of knowledge asset valuation from the bottom up: They point to software, patents and trained people, and then try to estimate the valuation of that, adding it to come up with a total knowledge capital. Unfortunately, that's not what value is all about. Value is the customers' demand values. It is a top-down issue, not a bottom-up.

Very few organizations today are willing to put on their annual report a verifiable number that is recognized as knowledge capital. Senior management is still focusing on the conventional, deadly stuff: the old, industrial age accounting. If there is any change in such attitude, management tends to add all kinds of fancy prose either in the reports sent to shareholders or in speeches. In this case, it becomes typical to hear statements such as "our people are the most valuable asset we have." However, when their statistics are reported, return on equity (ROE), ROI, or ROA is still what is reported. The knowledge gap in the organization becomes very visible here, as what is said and what is done does not hold together.

On the other hand, this very same senior management is always open to any new ideas that can contribute to the increase in value of their companies. They have a keen interest is increasing stock prices, and the stock market clearly recognizes knowledge capital. This is true especially in the United States, where stock market valuations of equity are over six times those of the financial book assets. Only in the United States are stockholders willing to pay more than six times book value for their stocks. The reason for that is often the amount of knowledge capital the organization has, which is added to the financial equity value.

If you are finding it hard to accept this assertion, just try to take any public traded company's knowledge capital valuation (KCV) as proposed by Strassmann—discussed earlier in this chapter—and then add it to the shareholder's book equity. You will find that it closely tracks the stock market. Not convinced yet? Do you remember when Wall Street paid almost 3000 times earnings for Netscape? Surely the dotcom era is over, but there are still many companies holding extraordinary valuations, and Microsoft, Nokia, Cisco, Oracle, Siebel, and many other companies are examples of it. The bottom line is: people have been paying and are willing to pay for knowledge capital, so why don't organizations really take advantage of it?

## Investing in Knowledge Capital

You probably have heard it before, but in business, do you know what the definition of insanity is? It is to repeat the same business strategy over and over again and expect different results! To illustrate the motto in this context, take for example an event that I personally went through as a knowledge worker of a start-up technology company couple years ago: while teaming up with the CEO at that time, and meeting with venture capitalists (VCs) trying to close a round B financing, I used to emphasize in every meeting the value and importance of our company's IP portfolio.

Early on, when I joined the company only a few months after its inception and prior to the close of its round A financing, one of my first projects was to devise an IP strategy that not only took into consideration our current and unique technology, but also the need for raising market and technology barriers for new entrants. I worked so earnestly on this project that by the time we were raising our second round, almost one year later, we had already filed five patents and broken up our provisional one into multiple ones, in a way they all intertwined with each other, making it very complex (and expensive!) for any of them to be challenged in court.

When I started working on these issues, we realized that the value of a well-thought product architecture was not the tools and technologies we were using, but the people we had and their freedom to express and create what they were trained for—the knowledge capital we had accumulated. Fortunately, our lead VC realized it, too: As a strategic move, we changed the name of the company, its core technology, and market. Our VC trusted that we knew what we were doing, despite all the appearances that we were being another victim of lack of focus and nonexecution of a business plan. They realized that if they disregarded knowledge capital because it didn't show up in the budget they were likely to make very poor and costly decisions.

### Measuring Knowledge Capital

As many companies evolve to this new knowledge-based economy, measuring knowledge capital is becoming increasingly important. Learning organizations will be able to create a sustainable competitive advantage only if they can successfully manage knowledge capital. The long-term success of any organization will come from their knowledge-based assets—physical assets may be important, but they are unlikely to be an effective competitive weapon as knowledge assets—such as:

- customer relationships
- innovative products and services
- excellent process operations
- skills, capabilities and motivation
- data farms
- information systems.

## Customer Relationships

For Alvin Toffler,[4] the customer is now a participant in the production process. According to him, the lines between producer and consumer have been blurred, as a result of a shift toward consumption. Under this new paradigm, it is the customer now that provides information as to what they need or want. Without that information, producers create a product that they can't sell and no one wants. Furthermore, the Internet has radically changed and enhanced the customer's and producer's relationship.

Consequently, customer relationship has become crucial for today's business success, and CRM practices will become even more vital in this knowledge economy. Therefore, any organization that reduces its customer relationship budgets also reduces its customer relationships and thus weakens its brand loyalty. Organizations must realize that customer relationship costs are hidden in all sorts of budgets, whether they are marketing, advertising, public relations or transactions.

Those organizations that feel that they can get away with smaller customer relationship budgets are only fooling themselves, in particular if most of the interaction with the customer is online. Online customer relationships may give a superficial impression of community and friendliness. However, it is in reality a very impersonal medium. Websites viewed from computer monitors lean toward being cold, lifeless environments. E-mail is informal but can just as easily be impersonal. When you have to deal with 100 e-mails a day it's easy to become automatic in how you respond to practically everything. Such practice just widens the knowledge gap between the organization and its customers.

Therefore, organizations should develop brand communities online. Now, beware that brand communities are as much an attitude as a structure. Brand communities should be the environments in which the company and the customer carry out an online relationship.

## Innovative Products and Services

When it comes to innovating products and services in a knowledge-based economy, senior management should step out of the boat. This is true especially for knowledge workers, including myself, as we have been far too introspective for far too long, so no wonder KM, and knowledge workers!, have had to prove themselves over and over again. We've been spending too much time rearranging the furniture in our home and not enough with the people who enable us to pay the mortgage, so to speak. Focus should be given to our customers, both inside and outside the organization.

During the past decade, most of the organizational change initiatives such as reengineering, organizational learning and TQM did not exclude customers, but they tend to de-emphasize their importance in practice. Unfortunately, customers, inside and out the organization, are very important in the knowledge transfer process, which in turn is the key component in bridging the organization's knowledge gap.

Unless we become skilled at bridging knowledge gaps, investing in learning organizations will never succeed. No wonder Stan Davis, the world-recognized business consultant, still believes that investing in building learning organizations is a self-defeating job. In his experience, professionals focusing on learning organizations spend an enormous amount of time talking about the organization and lose sight of the business.

The problem is that learning organizations will never be successful unless knowledge transfer is effective. People tend to meet too much, to present too much, to talk too much when they hit knowledge walls. That's what makes them so ineffective, and consequently, their KM projects. In the process, as pointed out by Davis, professionals find themselves running in circles and never really achieving tangible, quantifiable business results, thus losing sight of the business challenge at hand.

Therefore, the vision every knowledge worker and KM professional should have when developing organizations into learning ones is to successfully enable knowledge gaps to be bridged, in particular among the company and its customers, allowing knowledge to effectively be transferred. This process requires a re-prioritization of the business goals, where the focus should be giving to customers, not business processes, not group integration, or even bottom line, unless if directly related to customers. Customers no longer occupy the other end of the sale-cycle stick. They are much more integrated in any successful business organization, influencing the development of new products and markets as never before.

Nowadays, customers are no longer adapting to markets. Instead, markets are adapting to customers' demands. This doesn't mean, however, that companies need to be at a customer's mercy. Instead, and this is where the power of KM comes in, companies' relationship with customers should be one of collaboration. In the process of developing learning organizations, customers' interactions with the company should also foster a learning relationship. Don Peppers and Martha Rogers, of Marketing 1:1 in Stamford, CT, wrote extensively about learning relationships with customers, in their book *The One to One Future,* which I recommend you read, as they emphasize the need for companies to concentrate on keeping and growing their customers rather than merely accepting a significant churn as a business reality. As Peppers[5] (p. 56, 2004) so keenly states, "You have to manage customers and relationships, not products and brands."

In focusing on bridging the knowledge gap between the enterprise and its customers, information technologies, including data farming and mining and the Internet, can assist the development of this notion of one-to-one marketing relationships, which Peppers advocates. As knowledge stored in customers' info islands and corporate silos are bridged, mass customization of products and services becomes possible. Learning organizations are taking advantage of this KM strategy with great success. Ritz-Carlton, which maintains a profile of each hotel guest, and Levi's, which now tailors the fit of its popular blue jeans to the needs of the individual, are examples of organizations succeeding with this approach.

### Excellent Process Operations

As learning organizations reap the benefits of bridged knowledge with customers and internal groups, companies can now focus on improving process operations, so they can retain a greater share of the customer's lifetime business rather than just market share. After all, retaining existing customers is much more profitable than continuously spending resources on finding new ones.

By striving to achieve excellent process operations, the goal should be to improve dialogue with customers, as well as knowledge workers within the organization. Only through a continuous dialog, a truly two-way exchange of knowledge between company and customer and every employee among themselves, is the relationship strengthened and true knowledge—not misinformation!—flows. That's when customers begin to invest time and effort in the relationship, and their willingness to share what they really need from the company and the product really happens. At this point, the company can learn about the customer's experience with their products and services, as they explain what they need, so that the company can personalize its product and service offerings to meet the customer's expectation.

### Skills, Capabilities, and Motivation

While the general view about the inefficiencies of KM and the lack of skilled knowledge professionals to lead learning organizations in America and worldwide is still strong, the fact of the matter is that there has never been a time that organizations were so much in need of such professionals.

The point is that KM professionals lie at the heart of innovation. Skilled knowledge professionals, in particular knowledge workers, should be considered a source of cutting-edge research and development—a wellspring of vital technology, information systems, human behavior, and sociology, market and business knowledge. Knowledge managers can be a dynamic force inside learning organizations in an interdependent value system that strives to tighten its relationship and knowledge of its customers and their needs. Today, the company's success is becoming a function of the success (not satisfaction!) of its customers. KM professionals are best positioned to bridge the gap between the company and the customer than any other professional, because of their eclectic background and multidisciplinary know-how, so vital in understanding and reaching out to the customers.

Typical marketing groups tend to become customer-led, focusing excessively on the existing needs of customers. However, these groups often fail in determining what the customer's unmet and unarticulated needs are. KM practices are a must to motivate learning organizations in collaborating with customers and promoting active dialog that spurs innovation, enabling companies to create new and profitable customer solutions. Steelcase, for instance, capitalizes on collaboration with its customers by relying on its customer field test sites for insights about creating effective workspaces. Northern Telecom also capitalizes on collaboration activities with its telecommunications equipment customers in its activities from design to deployment.

I strongly believe that the most impressive breakthroughs of the future will not originate in complex research and development labs or in visionary executive teams. They will happen outside the walls of the corporation, with knowledge workers and KM professionals as catalysts, connecting the knowledge base of the organization with customers, wherever they may be found.

## The Knowledge Gap

As we try to work with the complexities of this fast-moving, interdependent work environment, how well do KM tools and business models support learning organizations in new ways of thinking? How well do these tools enable the bridging of knowledge gaps within organizations? How long can we reconcile statements such as "people are our greatest assets" with our balance sheets where they show up only as a liability and expense?

In any learning organization, the people are indeed a core asset, and the way their knowledge and intelligence is utilized is a very important key strategy for the company's business advantage. Nonetheless, the great majority of professionals are bound by golden handcuffs of business, financial and economic models and frameworks that only continue to pull them in very different directions. So, how long will organizations, in particular the learning ones, be able to cope with this disconnect between what their people know, their know-how, what they say is important, and the financial and economic models that drive all of the day-to-day decisions?

Today, almost all of our business and economic models, as well as our everyday management tools, are leftovers from the industrial age. Over and over again, I watch senior managers and executives try to move forward into new ways of working and managing only to be frustrated by tools and frameworks that are inadequate for the new economy. The many times I attempted to emphasize the importance of KM and to bridge many knowledge islands inside the organization and use effective tools to manage this burst of information flow, my efforts fell on deaf ears.

The bottom line is that, unless we find ways to work the emerging set of very different questions imposed by this new knowledge economy, we will continue to witness the failure of many businesses, including our own, and consequently, dive into an economic recession. Curiously enough, history shows that it is only during economic recessions that companies take the risk to innovate and reevaluate their business, their management and their position in the marketplace. Business reengineering was the flagship out of the last economic recession. What will it be for this new one we are in? I'd bet, the bridge of knowledge gap through KM implementations.

### Reconsidering Old Tools

Senior management and executive staff must realize that this new knowledge economy we are entering, as we also enter the 21st century, is rewriting the rules of business and forcing a radical rethinking of corporate value and business models. The old economy of the nineties didn't have the many perspectives of value and capital we now have in the new economy, such as intellectual capital, knowledge value added and balanced scorecards. The industrial revolution didn't have to deal with such abstract notions (at least it was very much so back there!) such KM and learning organizations. But I strong believe that the notions of value and capital we are trying to cope with today is only the starting point of a major business shift, where not even our standardized analytical tools will not be sufficient to understand the complexities of value creation, preservation and transfer.

In my opinion, in order to be successful, organizations must be able to incorporate intangibles and intellectual capital in the way they do business, leaving behind the Cartesian mechanistic view of the economy and business, so much based on Newtonian physics. In the new knowledge economy, a more dynamic interconnected view based on insights gleaned from quantum physics, chaos and complexity theory, behavioral science, and living systems must be adopted. As Verna Allee long ago already asserted,[6] "the economic and business world is struggling to translate this new understanding of life that has emerged in recent years in terms of what it means for the way we do our work and how we manage organizations. We long to heal the split between the strong human values we hold dear and old business models where they are irrelevant."

To be effective, the major challenge knowledge workers face today is in trying to lead companies in adopting these new ideas and yet, finding themselves living the paradox of having their feet in two worlds: one foot is still stuck in the several decades old corporate world of management practice, and the other foot stands in the cloudy and fast-moving new waters of intangible assets and knowledge as the base for this new economic foundation of organizations and companies.

Unfortunately, a lot of what upper management thinks and does stems from old ways of thinking and an old mechanistic engineering-based approach, which means knowledge workers will have a tough time in convincing the executive group to rethink their way of doing business. Senior management and the executive staff are still unconsciously trying to stretch their old perspectives and tools to encompass new ideas, but as you might expect, they are not getting the results they expected. Many do not realize that the fundamental principles underlying intangibles and the knowledge economy are dramatically different from the way they have traditionally thought about how value is created and what makes organizations successful.

The major challenge here is that business professionals never had to deal with and manage knowledge as they do today. Knowledge has never been as prevalent, both on customers and suppliers, as it is today. Knowledge simply does not behave like natural resources. Knowledge and ideas can replicate and multiply endlessly, but material resources cannot. Natural resources deplete with use, but a knowledge resource is expanded with use—and sharing knowledge allows both parties to not only retain the resource, but also to amplify and expand it through the exchange process itself.

Further, the business practices and management principles that we are learning to operate by are very different as well. The industrial era enterprise models are no longer adequate to meet the dynamic conditions of an ever-changing world market. Knowledge intensive enterprises are calling forth a new approach to work, organizations, accounting, and business. In addition, there is a definite progression toward thinking about the enterprise from a more sociological perspective. To say the least, there is a strong appreciation from several companies, for what is known today as communities of practice. Companies such as British Petroleum, Buckman Laboratories, Chevron, General Motors, Hewlett Packard, Johnson & Johnson, Pillsbury, The World Bank, and the big consulting groups, among others, are all achieving outstanding business results by focusing on these internal communities.

### Turning Knowledge into Action

In this new knowledge economy, the best KM application in the world will not be enough to completely meet the challenge you have in turning knowledge into action. A KM application can help you in collecting, organizing, and sharing information among knowledge workers, thus promoting collaboration. But where its true value lies is in unearthing the real problems that we were probably aware of at the outset of our KM projects but were unable or too afraid to challenge head-on.

KM implementations can only be successful if contributors care about it and are motivated to own the content in the first place. In order to do this the content needs to become an inextricable part of their daily working lives, and KM implementation will not be enough. We need systems and ways of organizing knowledge that reflect the incredible diversity of people and ways in which they interact within the business itself. Knowledge sharing and management technologies are no longer enough.

Without a doubt, KM systems have helped organizations to bring order to the chaos of complete free-structure and nondistributed knowledge content mismanagement. Previously, knowledge would be anywhere, in any form, created by unknown sources and with unknown use and control over its lifecycle. To fix this, most KM implementations have applied a rigid rule of control where compliance to rules set centrally is foremost and the flexibility to react to the all-too-frequent exceptions that break the rules goes unsupported.

To effectively turn knowledge into action we must get to a point where KM systems will work with people's quirks, strengths, weaknesses, shortcomings and specific variances of style and use of IT tools before we can realistically expect buy-in from knowledge workers to the idea of total knowledge sharing and collaboration within the organization. Demanding that people use a template view of their knowledge creation and delivery and insisting that all knowledge workers adhere to this is merely a great way to let some people shine whilst others just lose interest and give up contributing their knowledge. Somehow we have to embrace the unstructured, and at times downright chaotic, knowledge–information–knowledge cycle, which I dubbed *the knowledge tornado.*

Current KM approaches are a great start. These approaches allow learning organizations to put rules around the things we know about, and encourage knowledge workers to create more of the things we already understand, thus tapping into this precious tacit knowledge in everyone's mind. What these systems absolutely don't do is allow learning organizations to grow outside of what they already know and understand, into areas of business and intelligence that may actually be of massive benefit. It's those areas of "uncharted and dynamic knowledge" that will allow learning organizations to become innovators rather than knowledge producers operating in a merely sausage-factory manner.

Another challenge is with regard to teamwork. Turning knowledge into action requires collaboration. However, in my view, collaboration is a fiction, a verbal convenience, rather than a useful description of how people at organizations cooperate and collaborate to create value. I'm not alone. Michael Schrage, in his book *No More Teams!*,[7] writes that the word team has been "so politicized, so ensnared in the pathology of the organization, that we don't really know what it means anymore." Schrage contends that we have become so obsessed with the composition of the team and the capabilities of its individual members that we have lost sight of how innovation really happens.

Therefore, in line with Schrage's thinking, I strongly believe that knowledge can only effectively be turned into action through innovation, and innovation requires what Schrage calls "cutting-edge teams," which are composed of knowledge workers drawn to innovative prototypes. Thus, creative collaboration becomes essential for business strategies and innovation. In this context, collaboration is not about communication. Effective collaboration does require successful communication, but it can only be achieved through the creation and maintenance of a place where the people can freely interact with each other, play and represent models of their ideas. This is what Schrage called shared space, which is key for the creation of shared understandings, an extension of knowledge sharing.

### Strategies for Bridging the Knowledge Gap

One of the major obstacles in developing strategies for bridging the knowledge gap inside an organization is that knowledge in itself is very complex. The many artificial intelligence initiatives of the 1970s, as well as the data mining and warehouse of the 1990s, showed us that we couldn't easily package knowledge into a black box and have it perform miracles. Moreover, many KM professionals are mistakenly confusing the concept of knowledge for information. Information is very important to any learning organization, and IT plays a major role in collecting, cataloging, and sharing the banks of information residing in data warehousing silos. But managing knowledge, in particular the tacit kind is not an easy task.

Often, the most valuable resource any successful organization has today is the knowledge in the minds of its people and its customers. So, how can we attempt to capture such knowledge, and subsequently transfer it? First, let's take a look at two typical and complementary approaches used today:

- Knowledge Conversion—This is one of the most typical attempts, influenced by IT organizations and CTOs assuming KM roles, to convert tacit knowledge into a more explicit form, through documents, processes, databases, and so on. This so-called decanting of human capital into a structural capital is the main emphasis of many European and U.S. knowledge projects.

- Tacit Knowledge Enhancement—This is an attempt to promote and generate tacit knowledge flow through enhanced human interactions. The idea is to facilitate the diffusion of knowledge around the organization, preventing it from being held inside the minds of a few.

It is important to observe that some of the fastest and most successful learning organizations heavily rely on KM tools and practices for competitive advantage. Tetra Pak Converting Technologies also takes advantage of this strategy by developing learning networks, where people from across the organization, update and develop their expertise in key technologies such as laminating and printing. The company understands that knowledge sharing is very important for innovation. Thus, they develop innovation workshops, expert and learning networks, as well as communities of practice.

Tetra Pak is only an example, among many, of organizations that exhibit best practice in knowledge innovation, but all of them show a number of recurring characteristics, including:

- Clear and explicit vision of their business strategy—Does your organization have a clear vision of your business strategy? Is the knowledge strategy something separate or is it simply another layer or view of existing business strategy? How does knowledge or know-how add value to your business strategy? Conversely, what exploitable knowledge products, processes, or expertise emanate from your business strategy?
- Understanding of what knowledge is—It is very important that your organization understands the knowledge advantage. Thus, you must discuss knowledge in your organization and make sure you differentiate knowledge from information, and that your people understand the advantages of nurturing and harvesting knowledge? Therefore, make sure the knowledge dimension becomes a key element of every product plan, marketing plan, strategic initiative, annual budget and personal development plan.

- A clear vision and architecture—What guides the business decisions in your organization? Is it the knowledge facet of your business framework? If so, how clear is the vision? Would an investor give you millions for your intangible ideas?
- Knowledge leadership—Do you have, or are you, a knowledge enthusiast, proponent of the knowledge agenda throughout your business? Does your CEO visibly reiterate the importance of your organizational knowledge to your business success?
- Methodical knowledge processes—Do you have a process methodology for capturing, organizing, and sharing knowledge throughout your organization? Do these processes enhance the creation of knowledge and innovation? Do you have policies and procedures to protect your knowledge assets?
- Proficient hard and soft knowledge infrastructures—Can the people in your organization readily communicate and access each other, as well as share information over the network? Do these networks extend outside the organization to reach supply chain and distribution channels, as well as partners and customers? Can you find what or who you want quickly and efficiently? Does your organization's culture promote innovation and learning? Are your organization's structures flexible and adaptive? Are your personnel systems geared to recognizing and rewarding individual and team knowledge contributions?
- Appropriate and realistic bottom line measures—Is the contribution of knowledge rewarded? Are intangible assets valued? Are financial performance indicators balanced with nonfinancial measures that underpin value creation? Do you measure knowledge flows?

If you can effectively and realistically answers these questions, you have probably already developed strategic advantage through the application of knowledge, and are ahead of most organizations in the world in this process. If not, then you should seriously consider starting it. Just like quality-defined success in the last decade, innovation through knowledge will be a key success factor in this knowledge economy.

## Turning Ideas into Assets

More than ever before true learning organizations understand that the greatest source of innovation and creativity for competitive edge is their own people. Hitting at the foundation of KM, the success of these organizations is greatly influenced by how well the ideas of its people are tapped and turned into valuable and tangible assets.

As part of turning knowledge into action, people must generate ideas so innovation can take place. Hence, everyone in the organization must be able to think creatively. I don't mean the developers and engineers only, but all groups within the organization, including sales, marketing, administration, shipping, and so on. If you plant the creativity seed right, you will have a flood of ideas coming from everywhere in the organization. At this stage, your goal should be to harvest these ideas by creating an intellectual property strategy that is valuable to the organization.

## Planting the Seeds of Creativity

Planting the seeds of creativity throughout the organization is a very important step, as it involves not only encouraging people to share their ideas but also to recognize that their ideas could be valuable. Often, rewards and recognition programs are very effective to motivate the groups.

When someone in the organization has an idea, they can get one-half of a monetary reward—say $50, or tickets to the theater—for filing an idea registration form. If that idea turns into material for a provisional patent application of an invention, then an invention form is filled and the complementary reward is given. If the provisional application then turns into a full patent application, then the person could receive a greater reward, one that will not only provide recompense but also motivate others to put their creative hat on.

Encouragement to be creative begins with the right attitude. There are several steps to creativity that any learning organization can follow, basically including:

- Attitude—This first step begins with creating a positive environment where people feel grateful going to work every day and being part of a team.
- Expectation—People also need to have a level of expectation set for them. What the organization expects from them, to be creative, is very important in setting people up for success.
- Awareness—This is a vital tool for generating great ideas. People need to be aware of where they can tap for new ideas. Some of the sources may be customer complaints, industry trends, business challenges, and workplace challenges.
- Subconscious—Help your people to be aware and trust their instincts. Tell them to pay attention to their dreams, daydreams included! Instruct them to think of a problem they want to find the solution for right before going to bed, and tell them not to be surprised if next day, or overnight, they wake up with a solution for it.
- Documentation—Be it at the office or while sleeping, make sure to ask your people to document their ideas. They should have a notepad next to their beds, so they can document their insights and submit them the next day.
- Self-praise—Praise is also a very important part of idea generation. Make sure to motivate people to personally give themselves a slap on the back.
- External praise—Make sure to be quick to also praise those generating ideas by recognizing them publicly.

## Chapter Summary

The focus of this chapter is to address the importance of developing a knowledge capital mindset. It discuss the various aspects of nurturing knowledge capital at learning organizations, from initial investment in it to measuring and developing a customer relationship around it.

# CHAPTER 7

# Knowledge Gaps and the Corporate Instinct

Opinions vary regarding the best ways to manage during hard times. Some say a downturn is a great time to consider outsourcing, while others say it's the worst. Some argue for immediate cuts across the board; others suggest it's better to examine processes and projects in order to trim fat, not internal organs. Interestingly enough, hard times are always characterized by the presence of many gaps in the organization, the market, the economy, management and so on. The harder the times, more the number of gaps and their impact:

- Gap in the excess of inventory, compared with demand
- Gap in profitability, compared with levels of investment
- Gap in creativity, compared with fierce competition
- Gap in skilled personnel and management, compared with eminent need for downsizing, layoffs and employee loyalty; and the list goes on….

Corporate gaps, no matter their nature, are always a challenge for management and the organization as a whole. However, for learning organizations, gaps can and should be opportunities to transcend, to renew and reinvent themselves. As discussed throughout this book, although organizations must learn to deal with the constant "move of the cheese," they will be better-off learning to constantly reinvent, re-create their own cheese. By doing so, learning organizations will be actually moving the market's cheese; for sure, it's the competitor's cheese. Call it disruptive technology, or strategy, today, organizations must be ready to view the everyday business challenges coming their way as a necessary gap. After all, such gaps are for sure inevitable.

This chapter introduces the notion of learning organizations feeding on gaps such as the ones listed above, and many others, as a necessary competitive advantage, as a way to transcend them and disrupt the status quo of their competitors and the business landscape. In the process, due to their very disruptive and unprecedented nature, the only way organizations can deal with gaps is by trusting their very own corporate instinct. If they were to rely on any other form of information other than that, they would only be repeating the so-called reengineering cycle. As a result, instead of transcending their corporate culture and know-how, they would be simply readapting to whatever model is known as "best practices" at the time, losing their edge, becoming conformant.

## Outsourcing: Are You Creating Another Gap?

Outsourcing can bring tangible benefits to any organization. It is typically the quickest response to any nonanticipated new gap in the organization, as well as the most efficient in quickly addressing and (hopefully!) ending a gap. But opting for outsourcing too quickly has a lot in common with taking a painkiller when something hurts, without bothering to identify the real source of the problem. Unfortunately, if not carefully considered, outsourcing promotes a lack of trust in the organization's instinct.

Any organization, as any human being, has its own instinct, something we Christians call Spirit. To ignore such corporate instinct, is the same as Christians ignoring the Spirit. It means you are definitely in danger and heading for trouble. Outsourcing has too many issues around it for any manager to do it quickly and right. If management does not stop and listen to the corporate instinct, the odds are that if they go through with it, they will not be able to outsource in a time frame that is meaningful. Once they do the due diligence and think it through, they will be about one year down the road, by which time the economy, and gaps, will have changed. They may find themselves ready to outsource at just the wrong time, just as those Christians that do not rely on the Spirit find themselves on the wrong path only because it was easier to enter the broad road than walk the narrow one. In business, just like in Christian life, the danger of outsourcing is that it often becomes a "quick fix," a "quick hit solution," that often produces adverse consequences. The odds are high that if a manager tries to rush through this kind of major decision, she/he will end up paying for it in the long run. Even if they do it right, they might not get the savings, or results, they want in the time frame they need.

## Using Corporate Instinct: Strengthening Your Processes

During an economic downturn such as the one the world is experiencing now, management tends to cut costs, in an attempt to reduce, or eliminate, the budget gap. Delays in project development or layoffs are very common, and are a result of conditional behavior, not corporate instinct. But isn't that what any competitor will typically do? However, if you were to use your corporate instinct, your gut feelings if you may, you should instead begin preparing your transition to economic recovery and boom. The challenge in tapping into corporate instinct is not intuitive and requires some level of paradoxical thinking. The challenge in "listening" to corporate instinct is that it invariably requires improving processes and automation. By improving process you are making an investment during a downturn to prepare for an upswing. Otherwise, when it comes, you may find your company very inefficient.

Trusting corporate instinct, as Koulopoulos, Tom, and Spinello[1] point out, enables companies to be successful time and time again. It is a result of deliberate action and can be developed. Actually, it must be! If you begin to rely on your organization's instinct you will find your organization acting beyond the confines of rational control, beyond memory, and systematic analysis. In this case, strategies are created out of a collective reflex. It is important to always improve efficiency and plan ahead, as traditional IT gurus will tell you, but more important, you should help your organization to tap into and intensify its corporate instinct, by enabling everyone to access this *collective corporate wisdom*.

Building on Koulopoulos, Tom, and Spinello's concept, corporate interviews and my own Knowledge Tornado concept, I confirmed that such collective corporate wisdom is an entity of the organization that can be negatively distinguished from an organization's memory by the fact that is does not, like the latter, owe its existence to corporate professional experience and consequently is not a corporate acquisition. That is why many companies do not react to fatal market shifts and sadly crash and burn: management tends to reject the collective corporate wisdom and opposes anyone that promotes or points it out, instead, wasting time on committees and PowerPoint presentations.

While the corporate memory is made up essentially of professional knowledge, best practices and other contents that have at one time been conscious to the organization and its staff, but which have disappeared from corporate consciousness by having been forgotten or repressed, the contents of the collective corporate wisdom have never been in any database or KM system, and therefore have never been individually acquired by anyone in the organization; they owe their existence exclusively to what I call *corporate heredity*. Whereas the corporate memory consists for the most part of complexes, the content of the collective corporate wisdom is made up essentially of knowledge. Koulopoulos, Toms, and Spinello confirm this, as they point out the importance of understanding that the knowledge on which corporate instinct is based is essentially mistaken by corporate memory. They go on to say that in a corporate setting, memory is most often associated with informal means of information capture and retrieval, a far less reliable basis of decision making than knowledge. Memory is selective and subjective. Knowledge, or more specifically a knowledge base, provides specific mechanisms by which to objectify, capture, and make available the collective experience of an organization.[2]

The concept of the knowledge, which is an indispensable correlation to the idea of the collective corporate wisdom, indicates the existence of definite forms in the corporate culture, which seem to be present always and everywhere in the organization. Thus, in addition to corporate memory, which is of a thoroughly knowledge-base-gathering nature and which it is only empirical knowledge (even if we tack on the corporate memory as an appendix), every organization also has a second knowledge system, an instinctive one, of a collective, universal (every other corporation has it too!) and impersonal nature: a collective corporate wisdom. This collective corporate wisdom does not develop individually, by every professional in the organization, but is inherited. It is created by everyone in the organization but is not owned by anyone. It consists of pre-existent data, the capital knowledge, which can only be turned into action secondarily and which provides definite data to certain knowledge contents.

## Disruptive Knowledge: Creating the Gap

Corporate instincts, as any human instincts, are highly conservative and have extreme antiquity with regard to both their dynamism and their collective reflex. Such reflex, when represented to the organization, appears as an idea or strategy, which expresses the nature of the instinctive impulse visually and concretely, like a picture. Now you know why after a new concept or idea is presented, the presenter typically asks, "if you got the picture."

In order to take advantage of corporate instinct you must understand that instinct is anything but a blind and indefinite impulse, since it proves to be attuned and adapted to a definite external situation, beyond the corporate walls. This latter circumstance gives it its specific and irreducible structure. Just as instinct is original and hereditary, so too does its structure transcend current management, market conditions or knowledge base.

These considerations naturally apply also to the corporation as a whole, which still remains within the framework of general business practices, despite the possession of knowledge, decision-making, and rationale. The fact that corporate business should be rooted in instinct and derive from it its dynamism, as well as the basic features of its innovation strategy, has the same significance for corporate business practices as for all other competitors in the marketplace. The dynamic nature of instinctive organizations allows for the free flow of new ideas. These organizations focus on their core competencies and not their core products, thus constantly competing not against their competitors, but against themselves. They do not allow the market or the competition to create a gap in their business goals, product/technology road map or revenues. The paradox is, these companies compete against themselves, creating the gaps before them and striving to overcome them before the competition does so. A great example of such a company is Microsoft, which drives the competition insane with the many products, versions, and renewed feature sets it releases over and over again, several times a year.

Disruptive knowledge, a powerful strategic tool, consists essentially in the constant adaptation of the primordial knowledge (or technology) pattern that was instituted in the organization. Disruptive knowledge creates gaps, challenges in the organization, as it introduces certain modifications to or insights into the original organization's knowledge. If the flow of instinctive dynamism into the organization is to be maintained, as is absolutely necessary for its existence in this new knowledge economy, then it is imperative that learning organizations remold their knowledge base into new and disruptive ideas, which are adequate to the challenge of the ever-present market. Organizations that are confronting gaps—changes—must first determine that they have the resources required to succeed. They then need to ask a separate question: does the organization have the processes and values to succeed? Asking such a question is not as instinctive because the processes by which work is done and the values by which employees make their decisions have served them well—corporate memory. Thus, disruptive knowledge can turn the very capabilities of an organization into its own disabilities as well. Relying on corporate instinct in such a situation can pay off handsomely. Collective corporate wisdom should be able to know if the process by which work habitually gets done in the organization is appropriate for the new problem.

Understanding the gaps created by a disruptive knowledge is a very important step in solving them. Not relying on the collective wisdom of the corporation can set teams charged with developing and implementing an innovation on a course fraught with roadblocks, second-guessing and frustration. The reasons why innovation often seems to be so difficult for established firms is that they refuse corporate instinct—or do not tap into it—employ highly capable people and then set them to work within processes and values that weren't designed to facilitate success with the task at hand. Tapping into corporate instinct, especially in light of dealing with disruptive knowledge, is not an easy task. Nothing estranges a corporation more from the ground plan of its instincts than its learning capacity, which turns out to be a genuine drive toward progressive transformations of corporate culture modes. The creation and re-creation of such disruptive knowledge, more than anything else, is responsible for the altered conditions of successful organizations and the need for new adaptations, which the marketplace brings. It is also the source of numerous organizational disturbances and difficulties occasioned by corporate progressive alienation from its instinctual foundation, that is, by its affinity and identification with its corporate memory, by its concern with corporate memory at the expense of the collective wisdom. The result is that most of today's corporations can know themselves only insofar as they can become aware of themselves.

## Corporate Instinct Is Old

Has corporate instinct always existed? Yes! Although some believe that corporate instinct is new, and that only individual instincts driven by their vision existed before, corporate instinct has more influence on an individual's instinct than the other way around. It's true that corporate instinct can only be leveraged fully when the tools and technologies for its development are readily available. But every corporation always had at its disposal tools and technologies, as those define the very nature of a corporation.

What does happen today that didn't happen before is that businesses are conducted at the speed of light. The advent of e-mail, Skype, YouTube, Tweeter, enterprise workflow, and other collaboration tools enables changes that used to take a full year, such as in manufacturing procurement, to happen now in less than a few minutes—as in e-procurement exchanges, such as eSteel, eChem, and ANX—through the use of collaboration tools, partnerships, and alliances.

But collaboration always existed, even if through primitive means such as interoffice memo or telex. The issue is that organizations never had the need to tap into corporate instinct, because there was time for fully rational decisions. But as the wheels of progress, in particular technological progress, increase speed and availability, corporations are being forced to tap into their corporate instinct in order to compete in time, to innovate and to adapt to new market demands. One way to keep up with it is through the development of community of practices.

## Communities of Practice: Coping With Disruptive Knowledge

The concept of community of practice is relatively new and has been used to describe loosely structured groups of people that share knowledge in areas of common interest. Innovative organizations have adopted this model to position themselves for leadership in the knowledge economy and to expand the benefits of corporate collective wisdom. Often, communities of practice do not operate on an explicit agenda. Instead, communities of practice members tend to share their experiences and knowledge in free-flowing, creative ways that foster new approaches to problems and promote collective wisdom.[3] I often try to organize communities of practice around the needs of the industry at organizations I am working for. I usually call them advisory group (AG). Despite the diversity of the group, we all shared a few common traits that besides dealing with disruptive knowledge included:

- Common interest or goal—AG was organized around topics that were important and meaningful to our membership.
- Common means to stay connected—AG stayed in frequent contact using e-mail listservs, Google Docs, Skype, webcasting or conference calls, and through more traditional approaches such as face-to-face meetings.
- Facilitated, not dominated—The role of the facilitator was important as it focused on recruiting and engaging members, not dictating content, which would completely block any instinctive activity.
- Management support, not control—Management provided tools and a supportive environment that includes providing members the time to participate and recognizing those that demonstrate an exemplary attitude toward community and sharing. The TAG set its own agendas based on the needs of members as they perform their jobs.
- Voluntary participation—Members choose to participate due to the "value added" in performing their jobs. Communities complement existing functions and organizational structures; they do not create additional ones.
- Willingness to share knowledge—Members are willing to share what they know, respond to requests, and collectively solve problems. They built trusting relationships.

## Sustainable Innovation Through Gap Generation

Successful use of corporate instinct enables sustainable innovation in the sense that what gets produced or created by the organization is sustainable. For instance, in the late 1980s, I used to be the CEO of an information system and technology (IS&T) consulting firm in New Hampshire, TechnoLogic. After the crash of the stock market in 1987, the United States experienced an economic downturn, so business was not easy and gaps were being generated almost daily. We decided to devote our human resources to innovating new products and services with office automation and internetworking in mind.

Despite the merits of collective wisdom—the term actually didn't exist back then, since the Delphi Group had not yet coined it—with everyone engaged in product and service development, the more we exercised corporate instinct, the less we had people to take care of the day-to-day needs of the corporation, such as making products, filling orders, or dealing with customers. In other words, we were all willing to think out-of-the-box, but no one knew what to do with the ideas and projects that resulted from such brainstorming, as they were all new to everyone, not present in the corporate memory or part of the skills set of the staff, which made the insights even more amazing as no one had any idea of how we got to them.

Clearly, there is a difference between the notions of sustainable innovation in the organization, versus innovation, one that is sustainable in the work process. Thus, the challenge to any organization tapping into its corporate instinct is that as a gap is filled—need for innovation—another one emerges, how should such innovation be implemented. As you rely again on corporate instinct and tap into corporate memory to resolve the challenge of implementing an innovative product/service, a new gap is created, as innovation then begins its institutionalization, and is thus no longer as innovative. The cycle restarts. The first stage deals with innovations and the corporate instinct in which they are produced, while the latter deals with the innovation process itself, as a component of the value chain, tapping into corporate memory, and which is independent of products produced or the sustainability of a firm.

Therefore, sustainable innovation must promote the sustainability of business; otherwise, innovation becomes only a great idea. The concept not only applies to outcomes in the product or organization sense of the term, but also to the process through which innovations are created. Thus, in my view, sustainable practices in business are utterly dependent upon whether or not sustainable innovation processes are in place, where the former cannot exist without the latter. Nonetheless, not always sustainable innovation programs lead to sustainable businesses, and not every organization, which practice sustainable innovation, will always be sustainable in their business affairs. The bottom line is that sustainable business is very unlikely in the absence of sustainable innovation.

## Nurturing Collective Wisdom: Attempting to Fill the Gap

Collective wisdom, as discussed earlier, can be an effective tool for solving the problem of knowledge deficit, or the underutilization of organizational knowledge. Hence, strategy meetings and other forms of brainstorm meetings where employees across the organization are encouraged to freely share their own ideas are powerful tools in nurturing collective wisdom that transcends the corporate memory. These meetings should cover areas that are largely determined by the specific needs (gaps) of the organization and may range from developing a corporate quality mission statement in establishing practical methods for empowering employees, creating a new concept for a product or service, and so on.

The main idea is to tap into the collective knowledge of the organization as a whole (memory) and its members, who then include their inherent tacit knowledge. Unfortunately, most of the knowledge contained in an organization goes unused, and many times gets lost, through employee layoffs and resignations, even before it is acknowledge and captured, generating knowledge deficits (another form of gap!).

According to TMP Worldwide,[4] it takes 1.5 times an employee's annual salary to replace that employee. This is due to several factors, one of which is the loss of unrecorded information and data. Lost information may include internal business processes, external contacts/relationships, and proprietary data. Knowledge deficit refers not only to know-how, but to codified data as well. Knowledge deficit is caused when employees cannot access:

- Databases
- Documents
- E-mail communications
- Expertise of other employees/outside sources
- Internet content.

Therefore, as gaps are created and the organization attempts to fill them, employees should have available at their disposal searching capabilities that enable them to search for codified data, as well as unrecorded, tacit knowledge ones. Such a process fosters collective wisdom, which in turn fosters innovation, one of the prime goals in tapping into corporate instinct. Expertise management, as information market accurately contends, enables the creation of knowledge superconductivity. For instance, strategy meetings can enable employees with business problems to tap into the minds of those experts who can at a minimum add to their knowledge, and may even be able to solve the business problem at hand. However, these meetings should be moderated and include a variety of themes and dynamics that encourage freethinking, commitment, loyalty, and wiliness to create. Hence, these meetings play an important role in ensuring that any effort in developing new concepts, in innovation, are supported by the entire organization, top to bottom. These meetings can include topics such as:

- Achieving unanimous agreement and commitment to a new concept by executives and senior management.
- Creating a comprehensive plan by which a new product or service concept can be implemented and become sustainable (remember, without sustainability, the new concept is only a great idea).
- Crisis/contingency systems (dealing with major gaps in times of chaos).

- Developing specific tactics by which new concepts and respective plans are to be realized.
- Establishing appropriate goals and benchmarks.

As well as these strategic and planning meetings, there are also some less apparent but equally important communication issues which can be addressed during the quest for collective wisdom, including:

- Developing high-profile actions that communicate management's commitment to change (creation of gaps) and innovation (bridging the gaps).
- Developing ongoing means for communicating progress of the strategy meetings and development of a collective wisdom process to both internal and external customers.
- Effectively communicating the collective wisdom to managers, staff and the entire organization as a whole.

## Few Focus Areas Where Corporate Instinct Pays Off

Corporate instinct is key in crossing new gaps and bridging them. It enables companies to unlearn as quickly as they re-learn, thereby pushing aside their own best ideas for new ones that meet the rapidly changing markets they inhabit. There are few areas, however, where corporate instincts can really pay off, including the ability to:

- recover from mistakes, both quickly and creatively;
- take considered risks and facilitate organizational change;
- communicate conviction;
- balance conflict tensions;
- promote intellectual prowess.

### Recovering From Mistakes, Both Quickly and Creatively

If well cultivated, corporate instinct enables an organization the ability to handle ambiguity, enabling the organization to recover from mistakes both quickly and creatively. Taking Wal-Mart as an example, going global isn't always a smooth process. In fact, some blunders are inevitable and Wal-Mart had to pull out from Germany and South Korea, not to mention the punitive moralism of Wal-Mart's Mexico mess. The Wal-Mart story is most importantly a reminder of the pervasive, even understandable, impulse within companies to ignore whistleblowers because they're so often time-wasters. And it's a reminder of why you can't turn your back on them. The real measure of success then becomes how, and how quickly, mistakes are detected and then fixed. Wal-Mart excels in this area—although not so in Mexico—and the result has been a reawakening of the kind of entrepreneurism and experimentation Wal-Mart has been known for in the early days under Sam Walton. In an instinctive corporation, the moment you let avoiding failure become your motivator, you lose.

### Communicating Conviction

Tapping into corporate instinct without communicating conviction predicts how likely the organization is to succeed, as well as how prone it is to derailing. Thus, as flag holders of corporate instinct, senior management must consider whether their organization fosters this competence, communicating conviction, or discourages it. To the degree that organizational climate nourishes this competence, the organization will be more effective and productive, as group intelligence[5] is maximized, that is, the synergistic interaction of every individual's best talents in the organization.

Take the example of GE's leadership development center, GE Crotonville, embodied by Jack Welch's vision for GE. Welch, then CEO of GE, effectively communicated conviction about his vision for GE, and the results are unquestionable to this date as we look at GE's performance year after year, and the caliber of its management staff. But looking at Welch's example, how can one break down his communicating conviction? Through a number of qualities that together inspire others to take risks, to trust their core competencies, and so on. It means a number of things, chief among them are confidence, clarity and charisma.

Today, more than ever before, executives in learning organizations must ride the knowledge tornado ever present in a knowledge-based economy. As a requirement, they must possess the confidence to make a difference. And they must be able to make critical decisions on the spot, sometimes in far-flung corporate outposts. They must trust the corporate memory and the collective wisdom of the organization, in particular of the senior staff. The ability to articulate a powerful vision for the company's future, to motivate others to put it into action and to act decisively is absolutely vital to any organization's success. But in a global organization, it is no less than a requirement.

Looking at how Welch reshaped GE during his tenure as CEO is a good example. He did it through more than 600 acquisitions and a powerful push into the world's emerging markets. But he did it also through the sheer force of his personality—and his conviction. No corporate memory could have provided data and enough conviction to achieve such a goal. It was, in most part, fruit of innovation, and corporate instinct at its best.

The mastering and leveraging of technology for business success is essential when competing in global markets and in knowledge-based economy, in particular knowledge technologies. But it is not enough. Despite the wonders of today's electronic communications, technology is no substitute for face-to-face interaction, emotional intelligence, and corporate instinct. That was why Jack spoke to every class at GE Crotonville and gathered his top executives there every quarter to review company strategy. It is also why he was known to fax off handwritten notes to his executives throughout the world. Beyond his unwavering conviction, Jack was also a master at balancing technology and technique.

### Balancing Conflict Tensions

The ability to balance conflicting tensions is a balancing act. Senior staff is increasingly being pressured to find new ways of organizing and managing the tensions between:

- Achieving growth organically and through acquisitions
- Centralized and decentralized structures
- Competing alone and in tandem with partners
- Global and local interests

- Product or market-oriented organizations and geographical organizations
- Short-term and long-term perspectives
- The rights of parent corporations and those of subsidiaries.

Clearly, these are thorny issues with no simple solutions, and a challenge in turning such organization into a knowing organization for the 21st century. In fact, some of these issues may defy solution. The challenge for the knowing organization, one that relies on corporate instinct, then, is not to solve these conflicts, but to acknowledge them and operate from within them. This means making a shift from *either/or* thinking to a broader, bolder both/and perspective. Again quoting Welch, from a *Business Week* article many years ago, "Anybody can manage short. Anybody can manage long. Balancing those two things is what management is really all about."

The management of a business structure that addresses the challenges listed above will always be prone to failure. In order to be able to adapt to the ever-shifting challenges (gaps!) so present in a knowledge economy, executives must organize without structure. When executives become aware of the corporate instinct, they morph their organization into a knowing organization, thus shifting the organizational structure paradigm into a fluid organizational structure. They would have developed and honed its instinctive power of adaptability and versatility through a heightened internal awareness, which is not locked into rigid organizational structures.

## Chapter Summary

This chapter discussed the knowledge gaps that are created at learning organizations and the presence of a corporate instinct at every organization. The chapter encourages the use of corporate Instinct to strengthen business processes and to deal with disruptive knowledge. Communities of practice and the need for nurturing collective wisdom is also discussed.

# CHAPTER 8

# Bridging the Knowledge Gap and Leadership Dilemmas

We all would like to think that business affairs are essentially rational; that they work like any other tangible interaction in this world, and that we should therefore be able to gain from them as they work to our benefit. However, we just need to take a look at the financial section of any newspaper, the TV news, the financial bulletins, Wall Street, to realize that business is anything but rational.

This chapter discusses exactly that, the leader's dilemma in making sense out of something that makes no sense at all, the business world. In having to rely on his/her own instincts, and the corporation's instinct, as the only tangible source of information to address the gaps between the old and the new corporate knowledge, and challenges of business strategies and practices, leaders are more than ever before faced with the imperative need to understand what I call the *science of bridging the gap*. In other words, to understand how the way they think shapes what they see, and how paradox and absurdity inevitably play a major part in their every action.

## Dealing With a Sea of Gaps

In order to innovate and effectively compete in the knowledge economy learning organizations must become knowing organizations; they must rely on the corporate instinct and tap into their collective corporate wisdom. The bottom line is, organizations must generate as many gaps as possible. After all, gaps are the seeds of innovation. Organizations must bridge these gaps, as quickly as possible, else chaos emerges.

Poor working relationships, internal and external strife, conflicts, misunderstandings, low productivity, and decreased customer satisfaction, lack of referrals, poor communication and low sales are all symptoms of chaos, all symptoms of gaps that are not being bridged, be it intentionally or not. The knowledge economy is characterized by constant and fast changes, and to be successful organizations and professionals must embrace change as quickly as it comes.

Nonetheless, to prevent chaos, or proliferation of gaps, executive leaders must embody the science of bridging gaps, of dealing with ever-changing environments and business landscapes, by developing a productive, team-oriented, positive atmosphere where good communication is paramount. Executives, and the organization as a whole, must not only learn to manage time but also manage themselves. Rather than focus on tasks and time, managers must focus on preserving and enhancing relationships and on accomplishing results. There will always be more to do than can be done by one person. If you are only doing the work of two people, you are loafing in your company. It doesn't matter whether it is two full-time jobs, four or twelve that you have to do. Your organization's productivity is the result of the trust the members of the organization have in each other. If you have the right trust, working relationship and environment, the work gets done!

Chaos, the end result of gaps, is a wonderfully evocative word, a formless void of primordial matter, the great deep, or if you prefer, the abyss out of which the cosmos or order of the universe was evolved. Can you think of anything that could be better calculated to set the creative energies of executives going than the challenge of forming order from the chaos of eminent changes in their business and organization? Many management and technology icons have responded to it and made remarkable progress in the last few years, but much remains to be done. The word on the street was that MBAs and other advanced management studies were redundant, that anyone can be a CEO and successfully run a company. Since the burst of the dotcom bubble that opinion is not encountered as often now. Overnight, executives learned that in the business world, especially one characterized by virtual enterprises and goods sold, executives, in particular CEOs, must also be information professionals, with the demonstrated ability to build a meaningful business within the void, which is being increasingly valued.

One of the most important lessons the dotcom era taught the executives was that you do not build a company in five days; you don't go IPO in a couple of months. For those companies that survived the first impact of the stock market crash in 2000, initially it was very hard to know how to break through the chaos barrier. Where could they begin? Savvy and successful executives answered by taking one first small step: developing a business strategy for what they would want to collect and preserve from their business, a laser-beam focus approach…if only they could find the wherewithal to do so!

You see, there was no corporate memory that could lead them in the right direction, and sadly, most of them did not know or rely on their corporate instinct. Thus, they started on a long, steep learning curve.

Unfortunately, schools are not teaching managers to deal with gaps, never mind bridge them when they occur. Although businesses are booming (great), when a hiccup in the economy happens, then it is doomsday. The problem is, managers, in particular in the United States and other developed countries, have been accustomed to believing the familiar bromides. When a manager, or any leader or executive, believes that their responsibilities can be discharged adequately by attending seminars or following simplistic formulas, then we have a problem. When such formulas fail them, not only do they get discouraged and frustrated, but also sometimes they totally derail.

Although these gaps are largely beyond the control of anyone at all, it is part of the chaos, or the eye of the tornado, as I define it; there is no golden rule to address them. Although gaps can be bridged, no bridges are created equal, and one must build his/her own organization's bridge. Further, as Richard Farson[1] so eloquently points out, while "years ago we talked about 'leadership,' the byword became 'morale,' then it was 'motivation,' then 'communication,' then 'culture,' then 'quality,' then 'excellence,' then 'chaos,' then back again to 'leadership.'" Along the way we were buffeted by buzzwords like "zero defect," "management by objectives," "quality circles," "TQM," "paradigm shift," "re-engineering," "six-sigma," and now "knowledge tornado." The confused executive, careening from trend to trend, cannot be an effective leader while believing in simplistic formulas and models, mine included!

Complexity science suggests that paradoxes are not problematic. Rather, they create a tension from which creative solutions emerge. This realization can shake someone at the core of his being. Charles Handy[2] for example, writes, "The important message for me was that there are never any simple or right answers in any part of life. I used to think that there were, or could be. I now see paradoxes everywhere I look. Every coin, I now realize, has at least two sides." Others see the concept of paradox as so important that they now define leadership as essentially the management of paradoxes. Paradoxes are defined as simultaneous or interdependent opposites.

## What Bridges a Knowledge Gap Is a New Gap

Rational and logical thinking have been responsible for most of all achievements in life. However, as these achievements were archived and access to them became possible, answers to previously unknown problems became searchable, thus limiting and constricting our ability to think creatively, to innovate. Just think about the automobile industry. Nothing really has changed, except for the first forays of hybrid cars, since the invention of automobile. Cars are still running on wheels and burning fossil fuel. Yet, from the invention of the wheel, cars pushed by horses, the first steam cars and finally the first engine-propelled car, not many years had gone by, but each of those stages transcended the next. The same holds true for the architecture and building construction.

I believe the problem is that we have grown insecure. Unfortunately, the price of relief from anxiety is the loss of creative ability. This is surely why we lost innovative teachers who felt there was no room for creativity, with the latest decade of change. At the beginning of the 20th century, inventors were bold, risk takers, and had to rely a lot on their own instincts, as there was not much memory (libraries, knowledge resources) available other than their own experimentation. The concept of dealing with gaps didn't exist, as life in itself was a big gap—no wonder the many philosophic schools, in particular the existentialist. Today's executives, for the most part are not willing to take risks. After all, many of them are afraid of what the Board will say, how Wall Street will judge them, what will happen if they are wrong, and so on. Instead of bridging gaps with another gap, they get immobilized. They become victims of their own contradictory impulses.

While delivering a workshop for a group of executives and senior technical managers in Vitoria-ES, Brazil, in 2010, I talked with at least three executives that clearly wanted to succeed in their business, but at the same time showed all the signals of wanting to fail as well. Everything they did, in their actions, carried both messages. One of them, from a major bank in Brazil, would be very excited about the prospect of automating certain decision-making processes within his organization. However, at the same time, all he did all day long was to cripple the project, by refusing to delegate, undermining his just-formed task force committee, failing to meet deadlines and stalling on crucial decisions.

Although back then I could not understand the situation—I, too, was a victim of not wanting to fill my own gaps by just accepting the most plausible excuse—what I realized over and over again throughout the years it that his behavior was not so unusual. Contradictory impulses, and Farson discusses the phenomenon extensively, are present in every project, every team. Thus every situation, every outcome, every achievement, can be both good and bad. That's why the science of bridging the gaps is essentially a challenge every leader has, the management of dilemmas, coping with contradictions while appreciating the coexistence of opposites is crucial to the development of a different way of thinking.

## Bridges Don't Last

It is evident that all things are impermanent, including the bridges used to overcome gaps. But didn't they used to fade, or change more slowly? No long ago, businesses were experiencing massive restructurings, re-engineering, and redirection. Skills and tools were needed for response to various impacts, to help us create rather than react. But now we are spinning faster, and the group change tools do not always seem to work. The reason is twofold: mistakenly identifying problems and believing that once a gap is bridged it will always be bridged.

Both assumptions are incorrect. First, many executives have difficulty distinguishing a problem from a predicament. Problems can always be solved, while predicaments can only be coped with. Spending time and energy on a predicament will only bring frustration, discouragement, and desolation. Most issues one faces in life, from marriage, family affairs, business affairs and so on, are complicated and inescapable dilemmas, they tend to be predicaments that make not a single option a best option, where all tend to be relative. Today's business environment is a lot like that. In this economy, management of information system (MIS) most often will not serve the executive management, either because these systems will be inadequate or because the executive will be computer naïve. Besides, how good is stored data if it is not real-time?

By accepting that all things are impermanent executives can take advantage of business tools that help them solve problems and accept predicaments, actually taking advantage of them, as those are very possibly the only consistent data they will have. Thus, some strategies to cope with such a paradox of bridging gaps are outlined below.

### Get Familiar With the Eye of the Knowledge Tornado Concept

Consider for a moment the outer limits of the tornado, as one goes through its outer stages of growth. It's chaotic, as it causes great devastation and change to everything it touches in the organization. Then think of the center of the tornado, the eye. There, all is calm, peaceful, and quiet. Think of it as your present organization status. For sure you will not be able to stop or even control the wind and the noise around the organization, be it competition noises, market shift winds and so on.

While you can retain your own center, and flow with the wind, with the tornado, that's the obvious thing to do. However, doing so is only to postpone the inevitable, the periphery of the tornado comes crashing your organization down, as in the example I gave of the movie *The Perfect Storm*. This is not a predicament, and has a solution. But the solution requires courage and a willingness to fail and die; crash and burn, as the Gloucester fishermen did in the movie, by a calculated and well-thought-out strategy that transcends the corporate memory and taps into the corporate instinct. Keep in mind that doing little other than that which seems absolutely safe could run much bigger risks than taking a chance. Risks are how we learn from our successes (not only mistakes!).

## Know What Matters

Michael Korda once said, "the first rule of success, and the one that supersedes all others, is to have energy. It is important to know how to concentrate it and focus it on the important things, instead of frittering it away on trivia."[3] The most powerful thing you can do at any moment is re-focus. Ask yourself: What do you want to achieve? Why is this important?

Keep in mind that gaps are inevitable; you will always have to deal with consequences of changes in the organization. And the fact your organization is learning only makes the advent of changes even more obvious, as awareness is part of the process. Once you learn that there is no face lost in abandoning all hope of completely avoiding gaps, you can much more comfortably get down to the task of managing how to decide which bits of it are worthy of your attention, and more important, which are not.

Your goal should always be of bridging the gap, which is the same as transcending, not adapting. Many people come to this epiphany when they have their second child. All the angst spent worrying about potential crises with the first child turns into considered risk management. With the first one it's *Oh my God—keep him away from that—it's got dirt on it!!*, and panic sets in. With the second one it's *Well, it's only dirt*, and serenity flows. Once you learn that gaps are part of business and transcending them part of the thrill, you then become a knowing organization, dependent on the next gap, so you can learn one more time and set a distance from your competitors. Much like surfers, you should look at gaps as the waves, the necessary element for a fun ride, full of emotions, accomplishments and lessons learned.

The trick is continually to assess issues by the amount of influence you have in determining their outcome. If you have no influence, your worrying isn't going to help it, so don't worry. If you have a moderate amount, do what you can and be satisfied that you've done your best. If you have great influence, then set it as a priority and influence away. No time to worry.

## Maintain Your Network

No organization is an island, and the 21st century will be characterized by partnerships and alliances. Any organization operates best when interdependent. Not leaning, but supported. It may be time to re-value partners, to re-assess alliances, to re-energize team consciousness in the workplace and community of practices. One of the keys to bridging gaps is the ability to tap into support facilities. Productivity almost invariably increases when it is delegated, leveraged, and pulled together. Hence, maintain your network of contacts:

- Begin using a contact manager—LinkedIn.com and Plaxo.com are great tools for that
- Keep all of your contacts—business, school, friends, acquaintances
- Be a source of referrals
- Let organizations know you don't mind being referred
- Build a select distribution list of supply chain, distribution channels and partners that you want to keep posted on what you are doing.

### Effective Leadership Does Not Avoid Conflicts

I believe that most executives may not have a problem with this, but as Wall Street gets more and more sensitive about the financials of any organization, there are executives that waste an enormous amount of time and energy in developing and maintaining a peachy mask. Today's business environment allows no time for that! It's time for empowerment.

Some areas you should be aware of include:

- Protecting the organization's interests from unscrupulous profit-making projects.
- Protecting organizations from unscrupulous employment of tax shelter schemes.

- Addressing privacy issues generated by the Internet and other new technologies.
- Monitoring the stewardship of the organization's assets.

## Strategies for Bridging the Gap

Organizational leaders are perpetually faced with a series of questions:

- In bridging a major gap (a change effort), should they drive the change, or build the bridge, from the top down or must it have bottom-up leadership?
- How would you make sure your organization is constantly innovating and at the same time delivering a standardized level of service?
- How would you encourage your senior management group to work as a team and at the same time not lose your star performers?

What these three questions all have in common is that they cannot be answered using solely logical methods. Yet, one of the bedrock principles of science is the universal applicability of logic. But an understanding and a facility with paradoxes are as important, if not more important than understanding logic. Although leadership is defined as the management of paradoxes, paradoxes are not managed in the way that problems are. Paradoxes have to be constantly managed, for they are never "solved" like problems. Additionally, paradox can be a critical concept to integrity. If a concept is paradoxical that in itself suggests that it smacks of integrity, which means it gives off the ring of truth. Conversely, if a concept is not in the least paradoxical, you should be suspicious of it and suspect that it has failed to integrate some aspect of the whole. Such premise is very important in generating and evaluating Thomas Koulopoulos[4] concept of collective corporate wisdom. Corporate wisdom brings wisdom to organizations by choosing behavior consciously and acting from inner wisdom, each of the workplace functions achieves higher integrity and higher performance on purpose.

## Chapter Summary

This chapter deals with the challenges of developing leadership at learning organizations which are in its nature proned to knowledge gaps. It emphasizes the importance of adopting the knowledge tornado methodology for developing effective leadership and strategies for bridging knowledge gaps.

# Notes

## Chapter 1

1. According to Ernst & Young.
2. Browne (1997), pp. 147–168.

## Chapter 2

1. Rebecca Barclay is President, Knowledge Management Associates Inc. barclay@knowledge-at-work.com
2. Davenport (2005).
3. Reinhardt, Schmidt, Sloep, and Drachsler (2011), pp. 150–174.
4. Mosco and McKercher, pp. vii–xxiv.
5. Congressional Research Service and Civil Service Retirement & Disability Fund. http://data.govloop.com/Government/Age-Distribution-of-Federal-Employees-Number-and-P/k5kr-j98h
6. http://www.integralvisions.com/bsmr.html

## Chapter 3

1. Charan (1989).

## Chapter 4

1. Garratt (2000).
2. trans. Frederick Goodrich Henke, Intro. James H. Tufts (1916).
3. Maltoni (2009).

## Chapter 5

1. Koulopoulos and Frappaolo (1999).
2. "What the CEO Wants You to Know," Crown Business (2001).
3. Garvin (2000).
4. Gates (1999).
5. Browne (1997).
6. Lawler et al. (2004), p. 5.

7. Welch and Byrne (2003), p. 169.
8. Kransdorff (1998).
9. Kransdorff (2009).

# Chapter 6

1. http://www.strassmann.com/
2. Stewart (1991).
3. European Management Journal (1996).
4. Toffler (2000).
5. Peppers (2004).
6. Allee (1997).
7. Schrage (1995).

# Chapter 7

1. In their book, "Corporate Instinct: Building a Knowing Enterprise for the 21st Century."
2. In their book "Corporate Instinct: Building a Knowing Enterprise for the 21st Century," ITP (1997), p. 6.
3. Snyder and Wenger (2000), p. 139.
4. http://www.tmpsearch.com
5. As Daniel Goleman (2000) defines. See also his latest edition when he emphasizes EQ as more important than IQ, by Bloomsbury Paperbacks, 2010.

# Chapter 8

1. Farson (1997).
2. Handy (2010).
3. Korda (2009), p. 78.
4. Koulopoulos (2011).

# References

Abecker, A., Aitken, S., Schmalhofer, F., & Tschaitschian, B. (1998). Proceedings of KAW 1998: Eleventh Workshop on Knowledge Acquisition, Modeling and Management: *KARATEKIT: Tools for the knowledge-creating company.* Alberta, Canada: Banff, 18–23.

Abecker, A., Bernardi, A., & Sintek, M. (1998). Towards a technology for organizational memories. *IEEE Intelligent Systems and Their Applications* *13*(3)40–48.

Abecker, A., Bernardi, A., & Sintek, M. (1999a). Proceedings of the 7th European Conference on Information System: *Enterprise information infrastructures for active, context-sensitive knowledge delivery.* Copenhagen, Denmark: ECIS.

Abecker, A., Bernardi, A., & Sintek, M. (1999b). Developing a knowledge management technology: An encompassing view on Know-More, Know-Net, and Enrich. Paper presented at IEEE WET-ICE 1999 Workshop on Knowledge Media Networking. Stanford, CA.

Allee, V. (1997a). *An emerging model of intellectual capital (or intangible assets).* Boston: Butterworth-Heinemann.

Allee, V. (1997b). *The knowledge evolution: Expanding organizational intelligence.* Boston: Butterworth-Heinemann.

Allee, V. (1997c). *The knowledge evolution: Building organizational intelligence.* Boston: Butterworth-Heinemann.

Allee, V. (1999). New tools for a new economy. *Perspectives on Business and Global Change 13*(4).

Allee, V. (2000a). eLearning is not knowledge management. *LineZine.*

Allee, V. (2000b). Reconfiguring the value network. *Journal of Business Strategy 21*(4).

Allee, V. (2002a). *The future of knowledge: Increasing prosperity through value networks.* Boston: Butterworth-Heinemann.

Allee, V. (2002b). *The knowledge evolution: Expanding organizational intelligence.* Boston: Butterworth-Heinemann.

Amidon, D. (1997). *Innovation strategy for the knowledge economy: The Ken awakening.* Boston: Butterworth-Heinemann.

Applehans, W., & Globe, A. (1998). *Managing knowledge: A practical web-based approach.* Reading, MA: Addison-Wesley.

Bair, J. (2005). Knowledge enabled enterprise architecture. [White paper]. http://strategy-partners.com

Baron, D. (1999). *Moses on management.* New York: Pocket Book/Simon & Schuster.

Becker, K. (2000). *Culture and international business.* Binghamton, NY: Haworth.

Bennis, W. (1997). *Organizing genius: The secretes of creative collaboration.* Reading, MA: Addison-Wesley.

Bolman, L., & Deal, T. (1998). *Modern approaches to understanding and managing organizations.* San Francisco: Jossey-Bass Inc.

Bookstein, A. (2000). Information coding in the internet environment. In T. Kanti Srikantaiah & M. E. D. Koenig (Eds.), *Knowledge management for the information professional* (Chapter 19). ASIS.

Bossidy, L., Charan, R., & Burck, C. (2002). *Execution: The discipline of getting things done.* New York: Crown.

Bounds, G., Yorks, L., & Ranney, G. (1994). *Beyond total quality management.* New York: McGraw-Hill.

Bourdreau, A., & Couillard, G. (1999). Systems integration and knowledge management. *Information Systems Management 16*(4), 24–32.

Brandenberger, A., & Nalebuff, B. (1997). *Co-Opetition: 1. a revolutionary mindset that redefines competition and cooperation; 2. The game theory strategy that's changing the game of business.* New York: Doubleday.

Briggs, D. (2000, April 21). Maximizing the knowledge asset value within the enterprise. *DM Direct.*

Brooking, A. (1996). *Intellectual capital: Core asset for the third millennium.* London: International Thomson Business Press.

Brooking, A. (1999). *Corporate memory: Strategies for knowledge management.* London: International Thomson Business Press.

Brooking, A., Board, P., & Jones, S. (January 1997). The predictive potential of intellectual capital. Paper presented at the National Business Conference. Hamilton, Ontario, 22–24.

Browne, J. (1997). Unleashing the power of learning. *Harvard Business Review.* (23), 34–41.

Brown, J., & Duguid, P. (2000). *The social life of information.* Boston: Harvard Business School Press.

Bukowitz, W. (1998). *Knowledge measurement: Phase three, global findings report.* Boston: Arthur Andersen.

Bukowitz, W., & Williams, R. (2000). *Knowledge management fieldbook.* London: Financial Times/Prentice-Hall.

Burstein, D., & Kline, D. (1996). *Road warriors: Dreams and nightmares along the information highway.* New York: Penguin Group.

Cabrera, A. (2000, October 2). Making sharing good for all. *Financial Times.*

Capshaw, S., & Kouloupoulos, T. M. (1999). Knowledge leadership. *DM Review.*

Charan, R. (1998). *Boards at work.* New York: Jossey-Bass.

Charan, R. (1989). Simplicity, speed and self-confidence: An interview with Jack Welch. *Harvard Business Review.*

Charan, R. (2001). *What the CEO wants you to know: How your company really works.* New York: Crown.

Charan, R., & Tichy, N. (2000). *Every business is a growth business.* New York: New York Times Books.

Christensen, C. (2000). *The innovator's dilemma.* New York: HarperBusiness.

Cohen, D., & Prusak, L. (1996). *British Petroleum's virtual teamwork program* [Case study]. Ernst & Young Center for Business Innovation, Boston.

Collins, J. (2001). *Good to great: Why some companies make the leap and others don't.* New York: HarperCollins.

Collison, C. (2001). BP Amoco's knowledge repository—connecting the new organization. *Knowledge Management Review.*

Comeau-Kirschner, C., & Wah, L. (2000). Who has the time to think? *Management Review.*

Cortada, J., & Woods, J. (1999). *The knowledge management yearbook 1999–2000.* Boston: Butterworth-Heinemann.

Cortada, J., & Woods, J. (2000). *The knowledge management yearbook 2000–2001.* Boston: Butterworth-Heinemann.

Craig, R. G. (1994). *Quality in the operational air force: A case of misplaced emphasis.* Maxwell AFB, AL: Air War College.

Cross, R., & Israelit, S. (2000). *Strategic learning in a knowledge economy: Individual, collective and organizational learning process.* Boston: Butterworth-Heinemann.

Cuthbertson, B. (2000, January). Tacit solution puts users in charge. *Knowledge Management Magazine.*

Dao, J., & Kristof, N. (2000). Bradley's fatal mistakes. *New York Times.*

Davenport, T. (2000). *Mission critical: Realizing the promise of enterprise systems.* Cambridge: Harvard Business School Press.

Davenport, T. (2005). *Thinking for a living: How to get better performances and results from knowledge workers.* Cambridge: Harvard Business School Press.

Davenport, T., & Prusak, L. (1998). *Working knowledge: How organizations manage what they know.* Boston: Harvard Business School Press.

Dennison, R. (2000). Bacon, eggs and knowledge management. *Virtual Business* 5(1), 12–14.

Despres, C., & Chauvel, D. (2000). *Knowledge horizons: The present and the promise of knowledge management.* Boston: Butterworth-Heinemann.

Dixon, N. (2000). *Common knowledge: How companies thrive by sharing what they know.* Cambridge: Harvard Business School Press.

Drennan, D. (1992). *Transforming company culture: Getting your company from where you are now to where you want to be.* London: McGraw-Hill.

Drucker, P. F. (1999). Knowledge-worker productivity: The biggest challenge. *California Management Review 41*(2), 45–53.

Drucker, P. F. (2000). Managing knowledge means managing oneself. *Leader to Leader 16.*

Edvinsson, L., & Malone, M. (1997). *Intellectual capital: Realizing your company's true value by finding its hidden brainpower.* New York: Harper Business.

English, L. P. (1999). Information quality in the knowledge age. *DM Review.*

Farson, R. (1997). *Management of the absurd: Paradox in leadership.* New York: Touchstone.

Ferrusi Ross, C. (1999). The role of IT: Subtle changes afoot for IT. *Information Week.*

Fisher, K., & Fisher, M. (1998). *The distributed mind: Achieving high performance through the collective intelligence of knowledge work teams.* New York: AMACOM.

Fowler, A. (2000). The role of AI-based Technology in support of the knowledge management value activity cycle. *Journal of Strategic Information Systems 9*(2–3), 107–128.

Freedman, D. (2000). *Corps business: The 30 management principles of the US Marines.* New York: Harper Business.

Freese, E. (2001). Proceedings of XML Europe 2001, 21–25 May 2001: *Harvesting Knowledge from the Organization's Information Assets.* Berlin, Germany, Alexandria, VA: Graphic Communications Association.

Garratt, B. (2000a). *The learning organization: Developing democracy at work.* London: HarperCollins Business.

Garratt, B. (2000b). *The twelve organizational capabilities.* London: HarperCollins Business.

Garvin, D. (2000). *Learning in action: A guide to putting the learning organization to work.* Cambridge: Harvard Business School Press.

Gates, B. (1999). *Business @ the speed of thought.* New York: Warner Books.

Gersting, A., Gordon, C., & Ives, B. (1999). Implementing knowledge management: Navigating the organizational journey. *Knowledge Management.*

Goleman, D. (2000). *Working with emotional intelligence.* New York: Bantam Books.

Goncalves, M. (2001). Proceedings of XML Europe 2001, 21–5 May 2001: *The Power of Cocoon for Knowledge Technologies.* Berlin, Germany, Alexandria, VA: Graphic Communications Association.

Graham, A. B., & Pizzo, V. G. (1996). A question of balance: Case studies in strategic knowledge management. *European Management Journal 14*(4), 338–346.

Grammer, J. (2000). The enterprise knowledge portal. *DM Review.*

Gray, P. H. (2000). The effects of knowledge management systems on emergent teams: Towards a research model. *Journal of Strategic Information Systems* *9*(2–3), 175–191.

Grushkin, B. (2000). Context dependency. *Intelligent Enterprise 3*(15), 29.

Halal, W. E. (1998). *The infinite resource: Creating and leading the knowledge enterprise.* San Francisco: Jossey-Bass.

Hamel, G. (2002). *Leading the revolution.* Boston: Harvard Business School Press.

Hamel, G., & Prahalad, C. K. (1994). *Competing for the future.* Boston: Harvard Business School Press.

Harris, K. (2001). Transforming the way organizations work [White paper]. *Strategic directions: Knowledge management and e-Learning, CIO magazine supplement.* New York: CMP.

Hatten, K., & Rosenthal, S. (2001). *Reaching for the knowledge edge: How the knowing corporation seeks, shares and uses knowledge for strategic advantage.* New York: AMACOM.

Heenan, D., & Bennis, W. *Co-Leaders: The power of great partnerships.* New York: John Wiley & Sons.

Hickins, M. (2000). Xerox shares its knowledge. *Management Review.*

Hildebrand, C. (1999). Making KM pay off. *CIO Enterprise Magazine.*

Jensen, B. (2000). *Simplicity: The new competitive advantage in a world of more, better, faster.* Cambridge, MA: Perseus.

Johnson, S. (1998). *Who moved my cheese?* New York: G.P. Putnam's.

Joia, L. A. (2000). Measuring intangible corporate assets: Linking business strategy with intellectual capital. *Journal of Intellectual Capital 1*(1), 68–84.

Kelley, T. (2001). *The art of innovation.* New York: Random House.

Klein, D. (1998). *The strategic management of intellectual capital.* Boston: Butterworth-Heinemann.

Korda, M. (2000). *Another life.* New York: Random House/Dell.

Kotter, J. (1998). Leading change: Why transformation efforts fail. *Harvard Business Review on Change.*

Koulopoulos, T. (1997). *Smart company, smart tools: Transforming business process into business assets.* New York: John Wiley & Sons.

Koulopoulos, T., & Frappaolo, C. (1999). *Smart things to know about KM.* Dover: Capstone.

Koulopoulos, T., & Palmer, N. (2001). *The X-economy.* New York: Texere.

Koulopoulos, T., Toms, W., & Spinello, R. (1997). *Corporate instinct: Building a knowing enterprise for the 21st century.* New York: John Wiley & Sons.

Kransdorff, A. (1998). *Corporate amnesia.* Boston: Butterworth-Heinemann.

Kransdorff, A. (2009). *Knowledge management: Begging for a bigger role* (2nd ed.). Business Expert Press.

Lawler, E. E. (1977). Adaptive experiments: An approach to organizational behavior research. *Academy of Management Review 2*, 576–585.

Lawler et al. (2004). *Human resources business process outsourcing: Transforming how HR gets its work done.* Jossey-Bass Business & Management.

Lawson, I. (2001). *Fast track: Leadership.* London: The Industrial Society.

Leonard-Barton, D. (1995). *Wellsprings of knowledge: Building and sustaining the sources of innovation.* Cambridge, MA: Harvard Business School Press.

Leonard-Barton, D. (1998). *When sparks fly: Igniting creativity in groups.* Cambridge, MA: Harvard Business School Press.

Liautaud, B. (2000). *e-Business intelligence: Turning information into knowledge into profit.* New York: McGraw-Hill.

Lowe, J. (1998). *Jack Welch speaks.* New York: John Wiley & Sons.

Malhotra, Y. (2000). *Knowledge management and virtual organizations.* New York: Idea Group Publishing.

Malhotra, Y. (2001). *Knowledge management and business model innovation.* New York: Idea Group Publishing.

Maltoni, V. (2009) *Strength in numbers: when PR partners with advertising and marketing online, you and your audience can have a much more engaging and interactive experience: An article from: Communication World,* International Association of Business Communicators.

Maurik, J. (2001). *Writers on leadership.* London: Penguin.

Nonaka, J. (2001). *Knowledge emergence: Social, technical and evolutionary dimensions of knowledge, creation.* London: Oxford University Press.

Pascale, R. T. (1990). *Managing on the edge.* New York: Simon & Shuster.

Peppers, D., & Rogers, M. (1993). *The one to one future: Building relationships one customer at a time.* New York: Currency/Doubleday.

Pfeffer, J., & Sutton, R. (1999). *The knowing-doing gap.* Boston: Harvard Business School Press.

Prusak, L. (1997). *Knowledge in organization.* Boston: Butterworth-Heinemann.

Reinhardt, Schmidt, Sloep, and Drachsler (2011), *Handbook of organizational learning and knowledge.* Oxford: Oxford University Press.

Ruggles, R., Meyer, C., & Holtshouse, D. (2001). *The knowledge advantage: 14 visionaries define marketplace success in the new economy.* London: Capstone.

Schein, E. (1997). *Organizational culture and leadership.* New York: Jossey-Bass Business and Management Series.

Schrage, M. (1995). *No more teams! Mastering the dynamics of creative collaboration.* New York: Currency/Doubleday.

Schwartz, E. (1999). *Digital Darwinism.* New York: Broadway Books.

Selby, R. W. (1998). *Microsoft secrets: How the world's most powerful software company creates technology, shapes markets, and manages people.* Louisville: Touchstone.

Senge, P. (1994). *The fifth discipline*. New York: Currency/Doubleday.

Skyrme, D. (1999). *Knowledge networking: Creating collaborative enterprise.* Woburn, MA: Butterworth-Heineman.

Snyder, W. M., & Wenger, E. C. (2000). Communities of practice: The organizational frontier. *Harvard Business Review 78*(1).

Stevens, M. (2001). *Extreme management: What they teach at Harvard Business School's advanced management program.* New York: Warner Books.

Strassmann, P. (1997). *The squandered computer.* New York: Information Economics Press.

Strassmann, P. (1999). *Information productivity.* New York: Information Economics Press.

Toffler, A. (1991). *The third wave.* New York: Bantam Books.

Tzu, S. (1984). *The art of war.* Oxford: Oxford University Press.

Useem, M. (1998). *The leadership moment: 9 true stories of triumph and disasters and lessons for us all.* New York: Times Book.

Useem, M. (2001). *Leading up: How to lead your boss so you both win.* New York: Crown.

Van Krogh, G., Ichijo, K., & Nonaka, I. (2000). *Enabling knowledge creation: How to unlock the mystery of tacit knowledge and release the power innovation.* Oxford: Oxford University Press.

Ward, R. (1997). *21st century corporate board.* New York: John Wiley & Sons.

Welch, J. (2001). *Excellence in management and leadership series.* Canada: MICA Group.

Welch, J., & Byrne, J. (2003). *Jack: Straight from the gut.* Business Plus.

Wheelwright, S., & Clarke, K. (1992). *Revolutionizing product development: Quantum leaps in speed, efficiency and quality.* New York: Free Press.

Yang-Ming, W. (1916). *The philosophy of Wang* (Frederick Goodrich Henke, Trans.). Chicago: The Open Court Publishing Co., passim.

Yoffie, D., & Kwak, M. (2001). *Judo strategy: Turning your competitor's strength to your advantage.* Cambridge: Harvard Business Press.

# Index

# Announcing the Business Expert Press Digital Library

*Concise E-books Business Students Need for Classroom and Research*

This book can also be purchased in an e-book collection by your library as

- a one-time purchase,
- that is owned forever,
- allows for simultaneous readers,
- has no restrictions on printing, and
- can be downloaded as PDFs from within the library community.

Our digital library collections are a great solution to beat the rising cost of textbooks. e-books can be loaded into their course management systems or onto student's e-book readers.

The **Business Expert Press** digital libraries are very affordable, with no obligation to buy in future years. For more information, please visit **www.businessexpertpress.com/librarians**. To set up a trial in the United States, please contact **Adam Chesler** at *adam.chesler@businessexpertpress .com* for all other regions, contact **Nicole Lee** at *nicole.lee@igroupnet.com*.

---